NATURE'S WITNESS

How Evolution Can Inspire Faith

DANIEL M. HARRELL

LIVING THEOLOGY / TONY JONES, SERIES EDITOR

ABINGDON PRESS
Nashville

NATURE'S WITNESS
HOW EVOLUTION CAN INSPIRE FAITH

Copyright © 2008 by Abingdon Press

This book is printed on recycled, acid-free paper.

Library of Congress Cataloging-in-Publication Data

Harrell, Daniel M., 1961-
    Nature's witness : how evolution can inspire faith / Daniel M. Harrell.
      p. cm.
    Includes bibliographical references and index.
    ISBN 978-0-687-64235-9 (binding: pbk., adhesive- lay-flat : alk. paper)
      1. Theology, Doctrinal. 2. Evolution (Biology)—Religious aspects—Christianity. 3. Nature—Religious aspects—Christianity. 4. Religion and science. I. Title.

    BT78.H295 2008
    231.7'652--dc22

                                                                            2008024698

08 09 10 11 12 13 14 15 16 17—10 9 8 7 6 5 4 3 2 1
MANUFACTURED IN THE UNITED STATES OF AMERICA

For Violet

More praise for *Nature's Witness*:

"For those who fear that either theology or science might become the ventriloquist controlling the voice of the other, this is a most welcome book. Affirming that both Scripture and scientific discovery must be heard, Harrell playfully and profoundly engages our most serious questions about life's beginnings and life's future. You'll want to pull up a chair and join him, his friend Dave, and Aunt Bernice in this important conversation."
  —**Joel B. Green**, Professor of New Testament Interpretation, Fuller Theological Seminary

"Many Christians steer clear of the evolution debate, fearing an adverse impact on their faith; others dismiss the scientific facts outright. But what if evolution is true? Venture into the maze of science, Scripture, theology, and faith with Daniel Harrell, and you will not be disappointed. It is a challenging and bumpy ride, but your faith will be informed, strengthened, and even inspired by the journey."
  —**Eileen Boye**, Instructor in Developmental Biology, Harvard School of Dental Medicine

"If you're a Christian who believes that evolutionary science provides an accurate account of the history and development of life on earth, you probably have some hard questions about what this means for Christian faith. I have these questions, too. How do we talk of a loving Creator while referring to random mutations? What does orthodox Christian faith say about the hundreds of millions of years of death and failure that preceded humanity's arrival on earth? How do extant hominids, descended from bacteria and fish, partake in the image of God and talk of everlasting life? We need a friend who understands these questions and who has the ability to address them knowledgeably while affirming our faith: someone smart and knowledgeable, but humble and faithful, maybe even funny. We need someone who knows what's at stake, but who also knows that our faith has nothing to fear in the face of the facts of God's world. And now, happily, we have Daniel Harrell's book. Full of wisdom, humility, patience, and good humor, it's a book I never dared to hope for. Enjoy it, and give thanks."
  —**Stephen Matheson**, Associate Professor of Biology, Calvin College

CONTENTS

Introduction to Living Theology

Tony Jones, Series Editor

I know a lot of theologians, and I don't know one who wants to hide theology under a bushel. No, they want to let it shine. But far too often, the best theology is hidden under a bushel of academic jargon and myriad footnotes. Such is the life of many a professor.

But in Emergent Village, we've always wanted to talk about the best theology around, and to do it in ways that are approachable for many people. Therefore, it makes a lot of sense for us to partner with our friends at Abingdon Press to produce a series of books of approachable theology—of "living theology."

Our friends who are writing in this series have academic chops: they can write the 400-page monograph with 800 footnotes. But that's not what we've asked them to do. Instead, we've asked them to write something they're passionate about, something that they think the rest of the church should be passionate about, too.

The result, we hope, is a series that will provoke conversation around ideas that matter to the Christian faith. We expect these books to be useful in church small groups and seminary classrooms and Emergent Village cohorts (our local incarnation). Likely, they'll raise as many questions as they answer.

And, in so doing, these books will not only tackle theological issues; they'll also promote a way of doing theology: one that is conversational, collegial, and winsome. Those of us who are involved in this series hold our own convictions, but we do so with enough humility to let contrary opinions shape us, too.

It's a messy endeavor, theology. But it's also fun and, in my experience, uniquely rewarding. So we offer this series to Christ's church, with a prayer that it will draw many closer to God and further down the journey of faith.

Grace and Peace.

INTRODUCTION

AT THE BEGINNING

Walking across the Boston Common one cold winter's eve, I was approached by a gentleman, somewhat agitated, who recognized me from church.

"Are you the minister who's writing the book on evolution?"

This didn't sound good. "Uh . . . yes?" I replied, bracing myself.

"Do you believe in the word of God? Do you believe that God created the heavens and the earth in six days, like the Bible says?" His articulation was semiautomatic—as was his tone.

I assured him that yes, I believe the Bible says that God created the heavens and the earth in six days. I also believe that rivers clap their hands and that mountains sing (Ps 98:8) because the Bible says that too. But I don't think that the Bible means six twenty-four-hour days any more than I believe that the Bible means that rivers have actual hands.

He worried that I suffered from delusion (which as far as I am concerned is never outside the realm of possibility). However, I reminded him that there are two types of delusion. There is the delusion that believes something that is not true, and there is the delusion that *fails* to believe something that *is* true. If evolution is an accurate description of the emergence of life, as science attests, then believing it alongside the Bible should pose no threat. There's no need to fear any honest search for truth because in the end, all honest searches for truth inevitably lead back to God.

Historically, religious faith, particularly Christianity, served as the loom onto which the discoveries of science were woven. It was within a Christian theological framework that scientific disclosure found its transcendent meaning. Descartes, Bacon, Galileo, Kepler, and Newton, believers all, saw their work not as replacements for faith, but as extensions of it. The idea was that the best of science and the best of theology concerted to give human beings deeper insight into the workings of the universe and, subsequently, into the divine character. Scientific discovery was received with gratitude to the Almighty for the wonder of his creation. Scientists, alongside the psalmist, would proclaim, "The heavens declare the glory of God; the skies proclaim the work of his hands" (Ps 19:1 NIV).

The balance between faith and science (or reason) was emphasized in the Middle Ages by Thomas Aquinas. Aquinas, building on Augustine, established a delicate equilibrium between theology (reasoning down from faith) and philosophy, analogous to science (reasoning up from sensory data).[1] Aquinas, unlike the Reformers who would follow, taught that human senses and rational faculties, as made by God, were competent for understanding reality, albeit from a limited standpoint. The limits were filled in by theology. Aquinas asserted that God acted through "secondary causes," creating the world according to his laws and then giving nature room to unfold in accordance with God's laws. Whatever was good science was good as far as God is concerned; science simply described what God had already done.[2]

However, if God operated mostly behind the scenes as the prime cause, then it wasn't long before people started wondering whether he was there at all. In time, reliance upon divine revelation gave way to human reason in its Enlightenment form, and soon the supernatural was rendered superfluous. As science advanced, particularly with the emergence of Darwin's theory of evolution, Christians reacted by retreating into a sort of Manichean dualism whereby science was demonized and faith grew reliant on a *super*-supernatural world where any ordinary explanation raised suspicion. With battle lines so starkly drawn, scientists were left to assume that any move toward Christian faith was akin to committing intellectual suicide. Conversely, the faithful relied on science for their medicine or the weather forecast, but much more than that was to attempt spiritual suicide. Let a spark of evolution in the door and you were liable to catch the whole house on fire.

The controversy between Christian faith and evolution is exacerbated by increasing mounds of scientific data that lend weight to evolution. Paleontology, biochemistry, cosmology, physics, genetics—you name the discipline—each regularly puts forth newly discovered evidence in support of Darwin's simple idea of descent with modification. While some people of faith choose to keep their doors closed, shutting out science is not necessary. Christian faith by definition defies human conceptions of reality (1 Cor 3:19). Its claims are grounded in extraordinary events that defy scientific explanation (most importantly the incarnation and resurrection of Jesus). But God is not only present where science is silent; he remains present where science speaks loudest. The expansiveness of the universe, the beauty and complexity of organic life, and the remarkable makeup of human consciousness—naturally explicable occurrences—are also interpreted by Christians as manifestations of God (Rom 1:20). Christianity consistently asserts that all truth is God's truth, implying that faith and science, despite differences when it comes to explaining *why*, nevertheless should agree in regard to *what is*. Why bother talking about God if God has no relation to observable reality?

An avalanche of books has been devoted to the controversy between Christianity and evolution. Don't expect a contribution to that debate here. There are plenty of other places where that conversation occurs. Instead, I'd like to look at Christian faith in the face of evolution as essentially true, as most scientists assert. Now I know that just because a particular theory makes sense of the way something could have happened, it doesn't necessarily mean that it actually happened that way. But if evolution truly provides an accurate description of life on earth, and things did happen the way evolution describes, how might we rethink the way we think about what the Bible says? To rethink what we think about the Bible is not to rewrite Scripture, nor is it to capitulate to Christianity's detractors. Instead, rethinking and reworking our theology in light of accurate data results in a more dependable and resilient theology. To be a serious Christian is to seek truth and find it as revealed by God both in Scripture *and* in nature. If God is the maker of heaven and earth, as we believe, then the heavens and earth, as science describes them, have something to say about God. Natural selection need not imply *godless* selection. To be reliable witnesses of creation can't help but make us more reliable witnesses to the Creator.

I do not approach any of this as a scientist but as a student of science and theology; and thus I approach it provisionally and not polemically. I'm not here to argue. As a pastor and a developmental psychologist, my own vocation has treaded the rocky boundaries between Christianity and science. The journey has made me alternately weary and exuberant, doubtful and hopeful, and at times torn. But it's been an important journey, one that I continue to traverse, not only along the trails of evolution in particular, but of science in general. I invite you to walk along.

You'll see a lot of notes at the end of the book. These are intentional. My hope is that as you read, your curiosity will be stimulated to the point that you'll want to investigate some of the scientists and theologians who've devoted their lives to these questions. Reading their works will carry you deeper into possible explanations and their scientific and theological justifications. My intention is not to repeat their work here, but to summarize what I think are some of the more plausible options I have found for reconciling faith and evolution.

My thanks to Dawn, my wonderful wife and editor extraordinaire. To Tony Jones and the Emergent gang who encouraged this series and this particular project. To Tim West and all the admirable folks at Abingdon. To Dr. John Free, Dr. Cindy Lu, and Dr. Joshua Mugford, who vetted the science. To Dr. Heather Curtis, Dr. Gordon Hugenberger, and Dr. Walter Kim, who made sure I didn't get too heretical. (Though in the case of both the science and the theology, all glitches and missteps that sneak through are mine alone.) And to Mike Ahearn, Dr. Lin Fisher, Matthew Lenig, Bill Pearson, and Joel Roth-Nater who gave the final draft a thorough once-over and offered their own valuable insights. I am grateful as well to all my family and friends who supported this work and are eager for their own faith to coexist with science in the happy realm of God's reality.

CHAPTER 1

HELLO, GOD?

The Religious Voice

I have no idea why I was asked to be the "religious voice" at a science conference. Well, actually, I do have *an idea*. A group of students from Harvard and MIT sponsored a gathering for their peers on genetic technology and society.[1] Because it was Harvard and MIT, the gathering drew a number of prominent scholars and practitioners. However, the invitation list was missing a theological perspective, which was something some of the students felt it necessary to have, if only in token form. Ergo my invitation. I do possess a theological perspective (a Christian, a semi-Calvinist, a closet Anglican). As a minister, I also have a religious voice (with a Southern twang). But I was a marginal science student. My problem in chemistry was that I never could remember which letters went with what element, or why. The math never made any sense to me. (How does $Al + O_2 \rightarrow Al_2O_3$? I still don't completely get it.) Physics was impossible and biology wasn't much better, though it was a little more tangible. In biology there were no indecipherable letters or equations, but rather Bunsen burners to light and formaldehyde-soaked frogs to disembowel. But aside from playing with fire and frog guts (which contributed to the D I received for my misconduct), biology didn't make a whole lot of sense back then either.

This lack of scientific acumen actually helps explain why I ended up a minister (that and a need to improve my conduct). Empirical reason and precision, while appreciated in pastors, are not required to "master divinity" (ironically, we ministers are awarded masters of divinity when we graduate from seminary). Theology is basically an exchange of ideas about ultimate reality, ideas that may be judged as right or wrong, depending on your point of view. Not that anything goes, but the boundaries are fuzzier when you're talking about an infinite God than when you're talking about something as singularly fixed as the speed of light. This may be why some scientists hold theologians in such contempt.

Why would anybody want to center their knowledge of reality on something so unverifiable and ambiguous as theology when there is so much else out there that passes empirical muster? If you're concerned about knowing absolute truth, why fool around with what very well may be nothing more than absolute nonsense?

I'll admit I've had my moments as a minister when I wonder whether I'm just making stuff up. People quote the Bible to support almost anything. I'll study and prepare sermons that ostensibly speak on behalf of God as if I had no agenda of my own, as if I truly know what God is thinking. I'll preach a particular point one week, only to preach what sounds like a contradictory point the next (though we preachers prefer to call these contradictions *paradoxes*). There is a good deal of ambiguity in theology (though we preachers prefer the word *mystery*). But sometimes I think I'm just playing with terminology. Does calling something *paradoxical* make it any less contradictory? A *mystery* remains ambiguous no matter what you name it. Theology operates contingent on faith. I do believe that ultimate truth resides in God. Knowing truth is therefore dependent upon God's revealing it. But I also hold that people are finite and fallen. Sin has a way of blurring our vision. Therefore even with truth, there's a limit to any human ability to know it entirely. (Though even as I write, I wonder whether I'm making this up too.)

This is not the kind of mind-set you want to have walking into a science conference. Science isn't much for paradox and mystery. While it can put up with contradiction (as long as its techniques are sound), it detests ambiguity. While there exists plenty that is yet unknown, that does not mean the unknown will stay that way. As a freestanding reality, truth is not dependent upon one's particular perception. A tree falling in the forest generates sound waves whether your eardrum is there to vibrate and your auditory nerve to carry it to your brain. Truth is therefore open to discovery and inquiry, not dependent solely upon divine revelation. Given the right tools, whatever may be known can be known (and what can't be known scientifically doesn't really matter anyway). Unlike theological musings, scientific findings result from lengthy and rigorous scrutiny with the goal of accurately describing reality. Theories are constructed specifically to be rejected if wrong. Science depends upon a strongly disciplined methodology with public verification and independent corroboration. Confirmed research findings compel agreement by the entire scientific community regardless of any existing bias. Ask a scientifically qualified scientist in Rome or Tel Aviv, Calcutta or Kyoto, what matter is made of and in all four cities you will receive the same reply, "quarks and leptons."[2]

By contrast, ask four religiously qualified people in Rome, Tel Aviv, Calcutta, and Kyoto about the nature of *spiritual* matter, and you probably will get four different answers, and maybe more than that. Theologians and ministers are not exaggerating for effect when we say we don't fully understand what we are talking about.[3] The fundamental ineffability of God makes any claim to full understanding necessarily provisional. In fact, for some theological traditions, the pinnacle of knowledge is *not* knowing.[4] Theological propositions are not intended to be proven or repudiated on empirical grounds. In Christianity, conformity with Scripture and tradition are stressed, but disagreements are often settled simply by starting new traditions and denominations. Faith is the determinant, with one's experience and perspective playing an important supporting role. This is not a bad thing, mind you, but it is definitely not scientific.

So, yes, I felt a little intimidated when I realized what I was up against as the "religious voice" at a science conference. And once I found out I was scheduled to speak alongside MIT Nobel laureates and Harvard National Medal of Science winners, the intimidation was overrun by sheer panic!

Make Believe?

You can't make up stuff about empirical data. It wouldn't do to tag data as a *paradox* or a *mystery* and just let it go at that. I had to go into the conference with something more. At least I needed to *sound* informed. So I raced to the library and checked out a pile of books and articles. I boned up on the basics of evolutionary biology, genetic research, molecular biology, biochemistry, bioethics, economics, medicine, and law. Some of what I read was scary. But even more scary was reading just enough to fool myself into thinking I had a clue about things others had devoted entire careers to learning.[5]

For instance I read how plants are genetically engineered to be impervious to herbicides and how insects are being made to attack crop predators. I read how other organisms have been genetically engineered to clean up oil spills and absorb radioactivity. I read about the major commercial role of genetically altered plants and animals acting as living factories for the production of organic plastics, pharmaceuticals, and organs for transplantation into humans. Pharmaceutical companies are also manufacturing human skin for use on burn victims and soon hope to do the same with other body parts derived from harvested stem cells that are coaxed to grow on polymer frames. However, the development, mass production, and wholesale release of genetically engineered life forms into the ecosystem could cause irreversible damage to the biosphere, making genetic pollution an even greater threat to the planet than nuclear or petrochemical pollution. We can clean up an oil spill, but it's hard to clean up a genetic spill since it's composed of living material that mutates and reproduces. Of course, some of what's being manufactured is intended to cause environmental and personal harm. Work is ongoing in many countries, including the U.S., to develop and stockpile bacteria and viruses as weaponry.

Most presenters at the conference boasted of the potential for good inherent to their research, asserting that it far outweighs any potential for harm. "Trust us," they implied, knowing that it really doesn't matter whether we do or not. Technology and economics are huge drivers of scientific research. It can feel as if the only boundary lines are ability and funding (or profitability). Science possesses sufficient cachet to press forward in its more questionable endeavors since public opinion typically tends to come around in time. Initially *in vitro* fertilization was suspect, with its outcomes labeled "test tube babies." But now IVF is generally accepted despite the ethical conundrums it presents (such as issues related to gene manipulation and embryonic stem cell research).

At the science conference, I was assigned to a panel on human cloning. Cloning was the buzz topic that day: the infamous Dolly the Sheep had just come out of the hopper.[6] Checking out the schedule, I discovered that my panel was set to meet in the main auditorium. I felt nervous as I entered. The place was packed. Spotlights brightly burned the stage where four chairs were parked behind microphones. In front of the seats were name placards: *MIT, Nobel Science for Physics; Chair, Brown Biology Department; Bioethics, University of Pennsylvania;* and then me, *Minister*. I took my seat and stared into a crowd I couldn't see because of the glare. I gazed instead at the glass of water on the table before me. The water was shaking, though that may have been me.

The moderator welcomed the audience and then invited each panelist to present opening remarks. What was our position on human cloning? The FDA has since declared cloned animals safe to eat, and some countries allow the cloning of human embryos for stem cell research in medicine. Screening of *in vitro* fertilized embryos for a limited number of diseases and abnormal development already occurs prior to implantation, as does the availability of human eggs and sperm from Ivy League donors online (supposedly making it easier for babies to get into Yale some day). But then as now, there is a moral consensus that considers birthing fully developed human clones to be unethical. This consensus against giving birth to cloned children has to do with the tendency among cloned mammals to develop inexplicable abnormalities as they age. There are psychological concerns associated with people thinking that a clone could "replace" a lost loved one or child. Also, there may be concerns that cloning requires no male involvement. Men aren't quite ready to become obsolete.

There's also a "yuck factor." Cloning yourself is disgusting. The bioethicist on our panel addressed this yuck factor in his opening remarks. He challenged the idea that cloning is regarded as unethical because it doesn't *feel* right. There's nothing intrinsically harmful or wrong with duplicating genes. Your body does it naturally in millions of new cells every day—and that's just to keep your skin healthy. He smugly asserted that eventually people will get over the yuckiness, just as they got over it with *in vitro* fertilization. So-called "replacement babies" will be as normal then as "test tube babies" are now. You'll see.

What did the "religious voice" have to say?

Stepping up to the podium, I cleared my throat and adjusted my tie, which felt more like a noose. I braced to be laughed out of the room. This wasn't going to be like it is on Sundays. Theological dialogue counts on an essential set of assumptions, such as the existence of God and humans' sense of virtue. For Christians, belief in Jesus as God incarnate (or at least in Jesus as the epitome of humanity) is also an essential assumption. These were not assumptions many in this auditorium shared.

My opening remarks argued against cloning based on a parallel between Jesus as God in human form and every other human being. Borrowing language from the Nicene Creed, I suggested how, *theologically speaking*, children "begotten" as a gift of marital love are somehow distinguishable from children "made" as cloned products of personal preference.[7] That Jesus was "begotten of the Father" instead of "made" as an act of creation distinguished Jesus and set him above every other person. Likewise, children begotten by human fathers are somehow to be set above children "made" as an act of replication by a mother with no paternal input. Begetting necessitates two people; cloning takes only one. Bearing offspring becomes the result of purely selfish motivation; a clone is an exact genetic copy of the mother. Cloning could not be the same as "bearing offspring" because a person's clone can't be his or her child. A mother's clone is her identical twin sister. Yuck.

I thought I'd made a respectable argument. No mass conversions occurred, but I was expecting there to be at least be some mild applause. Somebody in church would have uttered an "amen" if only to be polite. But I got nothing from this audience. I don't think anybody had any idea what I was talking about. It was too much of a *mystery*, I guess. However, one young man stepped out into the aisle and up to the mike. He had a question.

"Would a clone have a soul?" he asked.

He caught me unawares. I was prepared to argue that a clone wasn't offspring, but I was not prepared to argue that a clone wasn't *human*. I'd read enough to concede that genetically speaking, a clone would have the makeup of any other person. The spotlight brightened. The noose tightened.

"Well, that all depends on what you meant by *soul*," I dodged.

"What do *you* think is meant by a soul?" he replied, lobbing it right back at me.

I knew what I thought. But I wasn't sure what to say. Traditionally, theology holds the soul to be the immaterial, immortal source of human personality, that inner aspect of human nature that distinguishes people from animals. It's what floats off to heaven (or to that other place) after our bodies die. That's how folks generally talk about souls in church. However, advances in biology and genetics increasingly demonstrate that human nature is continuous with every other form of nature. Animals, plants, and people all apparently come from the same primordial stuff. We're not as different as we'd like to think. Furthermore, neuroscientists (who study the brain) now assert that whatever it is we mean by *soul* (or *mind* or *sentience*), it's not some separate entity connected to or in communication with the brain. The soul *is* the brain, or more specifically, the soul is a function of brain function—it is both spiritual and material. The implication is that people are not comprised of two parts, mind (or soul) and body, but rather are singular persons.[8]

As a minister, I know something about souls. But as a developmental psychologist, I also know something about mind-body continuum and neurological function—which is probably how I ended up on the invitation list for a science conference in the first place. (Just because I was lousy at science in high school didn't mean I wasn't interested in it.) At the University of North Carolina, uncertain about what to do with my life, I defaulted to wanting "to work with people," which meant majoring in psychology. This began a journey that eventually took me to Gordon-Conwell Theological Seminary, since I wanted to work with God too. I became fascinated by the study of human thought and behavior from both psychological and theological perspectives. I loved delving into the different explanations for human behavior, motivation, attitudes, and addictions. My fascination led me back to graduate school, this time to Boston College, where I studied psychology proper as a doctoral student.

Yet returning to graduate school, I quickly discovered that psychology was undergoing dramatic changes. Everything I'd learned in college about human thought and behavior as attributable to subconscious drives, stimulus responses, or enigmatic "ghosts in the machine," was now being attributed to the brain itself. Psychology was looking more and more like hard science than social science, more and more *biological*. Therefore, *theologically* speaking as to whether a clone would have a soul, I perhaps could answer that a clone would have personality but no soul. A soul (to follow my logic) was something begotten rather than made (though I could be making this up). However *biologically and genetically* speaking, the clone would have to have whatever the mother had since mother and daughter would be genetically identical twins. So yes, I could also say that a clone would have a soul.

But what I said was, "It's a mystery," and let it go at that.

The bioethicist seated next to me was visibly agitated. Younger than me, he was probably bucking for tenure, looking to make a splash by taking down a minister. As soon as an opening presented itself, he lunged: "There's no 'mystery' to any of this! Humans are humans are humans regardless of how they come about, and religious people are simply deluded to think otherwise! Wax theological all you like, but when it comes to reality, whatever we know for sure is known scientifically. And what we know for sure is that nervous systems are just like respiratory or digestive systems. They evolved by natural selection. So did belief in an immortal soul. For whatever reason, belief in an immortal soul must have conferred some sort of ancestral reproductive advantage that we simply haven't been able to shake yet. Maybe it made our ancestors better risk-takers on behalf of others in their tribes. To believe your soul lives on forever makes you less afraid of dying. Driven by the demands of a hostile world, natural selection utilizes whatever works to survive, even if what works makes no rational sense. The answer is not theological *or* biological. Theology *is* biological! A clone would have a soul because the very idea of soul is nothing more than a construct of evolution."

The E-Word

He had uttered the E-word. *Evolution.* He redrew an ancient battle line in the sand. Christianity and evolution have been going at it for a long time.[9] How are we to understand the cosmos and its inhabitants? Did we come into existence by accident or by God? Can everything be explained by natural cause and effect? If so, are not all supernatural explanations thereby rendered superfluous ? What becomes of God once he's no longer needed to account for gaps in the scientific record? What if evolution fully explains existence and reality as we experience it? Can we deny the data that appear to support it without denying reality itself? How will people with faith in God cope if a worldview that omits faith in God turns out to be right?

My antagonist made a huge sweeping movement with his arm, dramatically pointing a finger toward the sky. He affirmed that science will march on, relentlessly testing every assumption about the human condition until one day, the very bedrock of moral and religious sentiment will be exposed as mere sediment.[10] To imagine that a divine being exists somewhere out there is so enormously ambiguous that it can be nothing more than imaginary. Evolution has accidentally wired us with a need to see ourselves as something more than animated dust, something more than talking and thinking compilations of organic material. But the fact is that we are nothing more than an assemblage of atoms and genes, cobbled together over time by nature's unforeseeing processes, our minds having emerged as "something of a bag of tricks."[11] Human thought and behavior can be reduced down to a remarkable network of observable and explicable neural patterns. That's all there is to it. And the sooner religious folks accept it, the better off everybody will be.

What could I say? I couldn't quote Scripture. I couldn't appeal to church tradition. I couldn't say "that's your opinion" either because it was not just his opinion. It belonged to numerous others sitting in that auditorium and in universities and laboratories worldwide. Luckily, the Nobel Prize–winning professor seated on my other side had pity on me. He was a grandfatherly figure, dressed in his pro-fessorial tweed and turtleneck. He adjusted his spectacles and chuckled.

"He's pretty passionate about his position, isn't he?" the professor chided, nodding toward the still steaming bioethicist. Then turning to the audience, he spoke into his microphone. "Whatever is meant by 'the soul,' it is not solely a neurological entity. Natural selection requires interaction with environments; it does not operate in a vacuum. Culture plays a role as do other organisms and contingencies. Evolution itself has no stake in the existence of God. Science can neither prove nor disprove divine reality. There's plenty that awaits our discovery but also plenty that we know will never be known except by speculation."

So there.

Basically what the professor said was that things are more complicated than the bioethicist made them out to be. And since the professor was a Nobel laureate, the angry bioethicist had to relent. Afterward, I stepped over to shake hands with my antagonist. He glared at me with contempt. He stuck out his hand, but with plain reluctance and disdain, his grip stiff and unresponsive. He couldn't stand that he'd been made to share the same stage with a minister. What I wouldn't have given for some good, old-fashioned fire and brimstone, something nice and hot like the consuming blaze that the prophet Elijah brought down onto the blasphemous prophets of Baal (1 Kgs 18). Talk about singeing a condescending smirk off somebody's smug face. That would have done it. I bet he would happily have shaken my hand after that. Whatever hand he had left.

But there wasn't any fire from heaven. Not even a spark. He had his visible and reputable scientific evidence. I had my invisible faith.

All Truth Is God's Truth

The biblical author of Hebrews insists that "faith is being sure of what we hope for and certain of what we do not see" (Heb 11:1 NIV). But sometimes that can feel like such a cop-out. I know scientific findings are not the same thing as scientific interpretations of those findings. Even among scientists, explanations of data can differ depending on who is doing the explaining. But still, scientific explanations accord with observed reality. Granted, "we walk by faith, not by sight" (2 Cor 5:7), but that only means that there's more to reality than what we see. It doesn't mean we ignore what we *can* see. Faith is not fantasy. If faith is going to matter, it too must correspond with the way things are rather than with the way we believers want things to be.

Christians are fond of saying that "all truth is God's truth." I believe this is right. Consequently, any pursuit of truth, through whatever discipline we pursue it, will eventually lead to God. But it can be hard to appreciate this at the trailhead, especially if we've chosen to start at a trailhead that treats science as anti-God. What if, instead of getting all threatened and frightened by scientific advances, we viewed scientific advancement as new vistas for theological consideration, new mountains to explore? Sure, I didn't like the bioethicist's interpretations and attitude, but that didn't mean he didn't have his facts straight. If all truth is God's truth, a true read of reality would only buttress theological understanding. If God is infinite, doesn't that mean there is always infinitely more to learn? Even from someone you might not want to school you? Clinging to false notions about how God operates in nature only forfeits the opportunity to praise God for how he truly operates.[12] If "all truth is God's truth," faith needs to work with science. Otherwise, as I was beginning to realize myself, theology becomes not only irrelevant but boring too.

As a minister, why would I bother talking about a God who has no relation to observable reality? That would only make me irrelevant (and boring). If God has nothing to do with actual life as we live it, then ethics would be left to function solely on the basis of utility over principle: do it if you're able. If God has nothing to do with morality, then principles themselves would become solely self-generated and self-serving. If God has nothing to do with evolution, then its valueless assertions would be free to justify all sorts of aberrant behavior. Evolution was cited as justification for Nazi eugenics. More recently, some evolutionary psychologists have suggested that rape may be a "natural" behavior.[13] Without some system of faith and value that can address actual behavior and choices, it's hard to argue against this.

What good is belief if what I believe has nothing of real substance to contribute to the real world? Inasmuch as "the earth is the LORD's and all that is in it" (Ps 24:1), theology needs not merely to withstand but to celebrate and safeguard accurate scientific discovery as a display of God's handiwork within faith's framework. And not just to celebrate, but to safeguard too. Science is too easily tempted by its own sense of importance to abuse its discoveries for power and profit. Science needs values that theology can provide to funnel its work into soliciting wonder at learning and into serving the needs of humanity.

Later at the conference, I dropped in on a panel discussion about medical ethics (one without a religious voice). During the Q&A, a student stood and asked the panelists what role they thought faith in God played in ethical determinations. Dead silence. Did no one know? Later in the day I was talking with a biology postdoctoral scholar, a professing Christian, who admitted that in her own work with genes, it was easy to concentrate on the living genetic material with little concern for the broader implications. She said that she hoped once she established her place in academia or industry, she would be able to step back and have a wider perspective. I asked why it was important to see things beyond the reductionisms of scientific research if basic, atomistic explanations sufficed? I was baiting her for a *God* answer. Again, dead silence. I thought she'd at least say something like "the whole is greater than the sum of its parts," even if she couldn't name the *whole* with theological vocabulary. I thought she'd acknowledge the dissatisfaction of describing everything in reductionist terms. But why would I expect that? It's not like we ministers have done so great a job helping people integrate their faith and work, not to mention faith and genetics.

Over lunch, I joined a discussion on faith and evolution with a group of students who were members of a medical school Bible study. The issue on their mind had to do with medical research. If the evolutionary and genetic continuity between humans and apes is in fact as strong as the evidence shows, what makes it OK to experiment on monkeys but not on people? I responded that the reason we don't work on people (and the reason we don't clone them) is because people are made (evolved) in the image of God and monkeys aren't.

One of the doctors remarked, "You can't say that in medical school." What he meant was that anything that smacked of religion wasn't accepted as suitable rationale for ethical decision-making. I understood. My own involvement with medical ethics committees has been one where "spirituality" can get treated as a concession to the unenlightened.

Even though Christians will say "all truth is God's truth," most keep faith and science separate so that our faith doesn't get threatened but also so that our science doesn't get ridiculed. The division widens to the point where there's not even available language to bridge it. But what if the science these students studied as doctors was the very way in which God created and sustains the world? Wouldn't we want to talk about that?

Lessons Learned

My experience at the science conference made me determined to learn more about science and especially about genetics, the brain, and evolution. It also made me determined to learn more about God. But this time, rather than treating faith and science as separate pursuits, I determined to learn more about the Creator by learning more about creation. I resolved to fight the penchant to divide faith and science into nonoverlapping compartments. I couldn't worry about my faith being threatened. Besides, if I was wrong about my faith, I needed it threatened. I thought about all the times I'd wished God had revealed himself more clearly. Wouldn't it be interesting if he already had, but I just hadn't been willing to see it?

For some this represents a dangerous track. If massive amounts of science, with its evolutionary underpinnings, manage to account for everything you see and most of what you don't, why bother with God anymore?[14] This is the dilemma hundreds of freshman biology students encounter every fall. Many of them end up in my office wondering why they need God if science has everything covered. Sure, there's the comforting thought of a benevolent Shepherd, some plan for your life or hope for after you die, but what if such thoughts are no more valid than imagining you're a bird or that you have superpowers? You look at the universe and see purpose and design, but what if you're actually just imposing purpose and design in retrospect? What if you're only doing it to validate a faith you should be discarding anyway?

All of this swam through my head as I wandered around the campus during a break. The sky and the trees looked like they always had. So did the people strolling in the sunlight. But the stuff I had heard and discussed now made me see the trees and the sky and the people so differently. Quarks and leptons, evolution and genes—with these serving as the determinants of life and matter, what could I say about God? Just because I say "I believe" doesn't make what I believe true. I could be wrong. Could my faith be wrong too?

Outside I bumped into a computer scientist who had attended the cloning discussion. He said he felt bad for me up there on stage duking it out with the bioethicist.

"It wasn't much of a fight," I admitted. Though I did have better hair. OK, I had *more* hair. I was reaching for any positive I could.

The computer scientist went on to describe his own collaborative interdisciplinary research which had charted plausible steps toward achieving human life expectancies of a thousand years or more. It sounded almost biblical.

"What will people in your profession do once folks can live forever on earth?" he asked with a sly look of bemusement.

"I don't know," I replied, "but it sounds like we'll have plenty of time to figure it out."

He jokingly responded that one way to turn atheists like him into believers would be to simply name the evolutionary processes *God* and be done with it. I laughed back, but apprehensively. Some believers play this name game. Another tendency we have is to ascribe divinity to the things that puzzle or frighten us, only to jettison the attribution once alternative scientific hypotheses emerge. To say "I believe" becomes just another way to say "I don't yet know." This is seen in what's called "God in the gaps" arguments. Take something that research has yet to fully account for and call it evidence of God's existence. The idea is that God must exist if science can't explain it. But that doesn't mean that science won't eventually explain it. And then what do you do once God gets squeezed out of the picture? Yet despite what some scientists say, there's no reason to conclude that God has no role in the things science explains.

I do believe in God. He has changed my life and established my identity in ways that I cannot otherwise imagine. He has done the same with billions of others before me. I also believe in the Bible. It has survived the most intense scrutiny to become the text that tells the best story of who we are and why we are here and how God loves us and saves us from our sinful selves. It is the word of life and the word of hope. And I believe in science too. It provides a tangible and reasonable system with which to describe and understand the physical world. Science does not answer all the questions (nor can it); nor is science right every time. Humility is as important for the scientist as it is for the theologian.[15] Nevertheless, science does show with ever-increasing accuracy that we inhabit a world that did not appear in an instant. Science shows that we as people inhabit bodies that are made of the same stuff as everything else, and that these bodies most likely developed over a long period of time.

Evolution describes a creation where randomness and lack of direction appear as the order of the day, where an enormous amount of time, death, and waste are required to get from the beginning to the end. This presents significant challenges to the view that God highly values purpose, life, and economy. Can we be absolutely sure that evolution is true? In the strictest sense, no. No more than we can be absolutely sure that God exists. Science, like theology and all human efforts at knowing, is by definition tentative. Science operates on the proposition that everything we think we know about the natural world can be rejected if it does not meet the test of observation and experiment. Science always seeks to correct itself.[16] Theology at its best can do the same. If all truth is God's truth, to insist on a view of God that contradicts his creation is to imply that God has not revealed himself in his creation. Actually, it's worse than that. To say that God negates science is to say that God has misleadingly rigged the universe. And to say that is to choose to worship deception rather than truth.[17]

Chapter 2

I'll Be a Monkey's Cousin

Evolution Is Hard to Swallow

Once you start delving into some of the more obscure things science takes for granted, it can feel like stepping into a whole new reality. Concepts like a curved universe, symbiosis, and quantum indeterminacy become part of your vocabulary. Who talks like that? Nobody where I come from. My family raised me on the fundamentals of Americana: God, fried chicken, and straight talk. Education was fine as long as you didn't show off. However, too much education made you suspect. Residue of fundamentalist anti-intellectualism ran in the water. When I visited Aunt Bernice after earning my PhD, she said she was glad because now I could help program her VCR. We had a neighbor who insisted he knew a boy who went to school for so long that his brain got too big and he died. Despite the absurdity of such a story, folks in my neighborhood would hear it and nod their heads. Served him right for trying to learn so much. Thus I knew that attempting to explain some of the things I'd been learning was going to set me up for some trouble. Mere mention of the E-word made Aunt Bernice throw up her arms in vexation.

"So you think we came from monkeys?" It was more of an accusation than a question. *Evolution* was a fightin' word.

I assured her I didn't think people came from monkeys. More likely we came from fish.[1] Scientists have long deduced from fossils that humans and all other vertebrate land animals descended from aquatic ancestors. In 2006, a group of paleontologists, working in the Canadian arctic, discovered a crucial piece to the evolutionary puzzle. They found a fish with limbs, making it among the first fish able to crawl out of the water onto land.[2] This particular species (named *Tiktaalik roseae*) lived about 375 million years ago and looked like a crocodile, only it had scales and fins. An extended elbow joint where fins regularly protrude made pushing itself up out of the water possible. Scientists had been searching for such a transitional missing link for quite some time. This discovery ranked right up there with other fossils such as the first multicellular organisms or the first warm-blooded animals. Of vital interest to scientists was how this fish exhibited the beginnings of the basic human body blueprint. This fish's fins foreshadowed the human arms and hands that emerged millions of years later.

"Sounds like a fish story to me," Aunt Bernice mocked. I could tell she thought I'd lost my mind. Who'd ever heard of a fish with hands?

"It's not that fish were ever people," I said, "or that people were ever fish, or even that people descended from fish directly. That's not how evolution works. Fish are more like distant cousins. Really distant. We share common ancestors with them from way back in history."

"So I guess you'll not be wanting any fried flounder for dinner tonight?" she replied. "Couldn't have you eating your cousin."

This wasn't going to be easy. But that couldn't change the strong evidence supporting the interrelatedness of everything and everybody on earth. If you were to chart out the sequential history of all living organisms, you'd get a massive family bush with all sorts of species stops and starts, successes and failures. Yet trace the innumerable branches back far enough and you find it all deriving from common ancestors. It's not only in the fossils that we see the evolutionary connections, but in the anatomical and genetic evidence too. Development of body parts and matches across plant and animal organisms throughout history square with the way Darwin described it. It's pretty random how it happens. There's no obvious pattern that evolution follows. While evolution in general has graduated from less complex to more complex species, there are plenty of species that have never evolved at all. By far, the dominant organisms on earth remain bacteria, which are basically unchanged since the beginning of life.

What makes evolution so tough for people of religious faith to swallow is that you don't need any religious faith to swallow it. Building off evidence from across practically the entire scientific spectrum, evolution can explain the origin, development, and diversification of biological life without any reference to divine help. That the supporting evidence is so all-inclusive, far-reaching, and integrated makes debunking Darwin's theory difficult. That evolution fits so well across so many scientific disciplines is what makes it such a powerful theory. Once you understand it n light of the evidence, you realize that evolution simply does the best job at making sense of how birds, bees, dogs, and fish emerged.

"It's simpler to say that God made them," Aunt Bernice answered rather tersely.

Yes, but religious faith doesn't generate the abundance of fruitful and testable ideas for scientific research that evolution generates. Evolution accurately describes natural life and history, allows for detailed predictions regarding organic behavior, and provides an ongoing impetus for further scientific discovery across almost every scientific discipline.[3] Modern biology and medicine would be unrecognizable without it.[4] Whenever a theory is as reliable, constructive, and internally consistent as is evolution, you have a very strong reason to believe that the picture it paints is, in fact, a correct picture of how the world works.[5]

How can we know evolution is true? Strictly speaking, evolution cannot be proved. Science operates on the principle of refutability: everything we think we know about the natural world can be rejected if it fails scientific scrutiny. You can't necessarily run evolution through a chemistry lab experiment or a particle accelerator. Testing the truth of evolution doesn't work like, say, mathematically testing the theory of relativity. Supporting evidence for evolution is obtained more like forensic evidence at a crime scene or like hereditary evidence from a paternity test. You deduce from clues gathered and from observations made. You compare DNA and look for the similarities. Conclusions are based on what explanation best fits the findings. Do this enough and a clear trend emerges. Do it some more and the conclusions become unequivocal.

Genetic composition of various species demonstrates a strong correlation across species as well as a link to previous species. Genetics provides the ability to trace the order in which species appear. There's anatomical evidence of transitional species, like the fish with elbows. And then there's the corroborating evidence that predators evolve with their prey and parasites evolve with their hosts because the organisms depend upon each other. This order solidly correlates with the fossil record. Fossils line up in the same order as the genetic family tree. Their ages correspond with the ages of the rocks in which they are found. These geologic ages are determined by the changing chemical compounds of the rocks themselves.

Once you start digging into the evidence across so many fields of study, it's hard not to be persuaded. There's really no better way to make sense of the immense array of data than a very ancient and evolving creation.[6] Can you call this proof? Does this make evolution *absolutely* true? No. But it does make evolution very, very trustworthy in that across most every scientific discipline evolution best describes what nature displays.

How Evolution Works

Before burrowing too deep into the details of the evidence, however, it's probably good to understand how evolution works. What happens? Basically, every living organism (people included) is made up of cells, each of which contain genetic code. Almost every cell in your body contains a carbon copy of your DNA, which defines you as the organism you are. Over time, mutations in your code occur as a result of errors in genetic replication,[7] cell division, recombination (mom and dad chromosomes getting together), or traveling genetic elements called *transposons* that hop around inside your collection of chromosomes and genes. These changes can lead to the appearance, modification, or elimination of a trait.[8]

"So are you trying to be helpful or not?" Aunt Bernice suspected that I'd been reading too many books I didn't quite understand.

Let's say that down by the lake some bird's offspring happens to have a slightly longer claw or beak. Or it possesses the ability to catch fish to eat. Or it has thicker skin. Genetic variation (through both mutation and recombination) guarantees that every individual is unique. Inasmuch as these variations confer some sort of advantage—the longer claw fends off predators better or the longer beak gets at worms better or the ability to fish makes getting food from a lake more likely or thicker skin keeps you drier—survival is enhanced. And since survivors in any environment are the ones who tend to live long enough to produce more offspring, they're the ones who pass on their modified traits to succeeding generations. Before you know it, everybody in that environment with longer claws and beaks and the ability to fish survives and reproduces better than their counterparts without these traits.

"Well, if you're going to be out on the lake, you're going to need webbed feet and not claws, you know," Aunt Bernice cribbled. "I've never seen a duck with claws."

"That's because of evolution," I pointed out.

"No, it's because a duck couldn't swim with claws." She grinned and jabbed her finger at my nose.

"Aunt Bernice, if a duck had claws it wouldn't be a duck."

Chance and Choice

But a bird with claws could have evolved into a duck. Evolution is a two-step process. First, a modification in DNA eventually manifests in a trait or a behavior. This first step is a "chance" process; that is, mutation, in and of itself, is not compelled. It just happens. Ducks don't grow webbing between their toes in response to the presence of water. Birds don't develop longer beaks because the worms run deeper. Plants don't generate resistance to pests because the pests are bothering them. Mutations are random. Nobody knows when they're going to happen. For the most part, variation simply shows up as if by accident, not in response to an individual's needs.

Evolution's second step, natural selection, "chooses" among the various traits and behaviors that appear in individuals, "picking" which ones get passed on to the next generation. Natural selection picks the individual in that the one with the most adaptable traits naturally survives. If webbing helps you survive the water, you live to reproduce webbed offspring. If fur gets you through the winter better than your hairless cousins, succeeding generations will have fur. Darwin used the phrase "survival of the fittest," which meant that the individuals that possessed the characteristics best adapted to the circumstances and demands of their environments were the individuals that survived. Natural selection is "anti-chance."[9] Variations don't fit by accident or by luck. The characteristics that succeed have to be the characteristics that provide an actual advantage. Eyes, for instance, didn't just appear one morning on some lizard's head. Eyes are the outcome of generations of individuals whose increasingly efficient structures for vision allowed them to better negotiate the demands of nature.[10] These approximations toward full vision were modified over time as improved sight proved advantageous for survival.

Variation and Natural Selection

We say *natural* selection (whether this entails the preservation or the elimination of a trait) to distinguish it from *artificial* selection, better known as breeding. Let's say you're a farmer who wants to make your corn resistant to some annoying pest that annually diminishes your yield. What you do is find another plant that has already demonstrated resistance, extract some of its DNA, and insert that DNA into your corn's DNA. Reproduce and presto: pest-resistant corn. The only real difference between breeding and natural selection is time and opportunity. You can manipulate heredity to cause pest-resistant corn within one generation because you can control the breeding process. But for pest-attracting corn to beget pest-resistant corn by itself could take a gazillion years because you have to wait for a pest-resistant gene to show up by chance. Once individual corn happened to generate the DNA, which resulted in a trait that resisted the pest in the pest-infested environment then that corn would fit best, survive, and reproduce to make fit corn for the next season of life.

Of course, had there been no corn-eating pests, generating the pest-resistant gene wouldn't have mattered. Again, those who describe evolution as a game of chance are only half right. The first step, genetic variation, is a genuinely random event, albeit random within the limits of biology. (Biology's constraints are determined by the genes already present.) Because of the random nature of genetic mutation, most mutations result in nothing new (and those that do tend to be detrimental to survival). But even when something potentially useful appears, the actual usefulness of the random new trait or behavior has to be determined by natural selection. Indeterminacy (variation) and determinacy (natural selection) need each other. Random mutation provides the new characteristic, and natural selection selects or eliminates the new characteristic based on whether it helps the organism thrive. If you're a web-footed bird in an arid climate, the inability to scratch for seed or run from predators may prove detrimental. The same with being a seed-eating bird with a short seed-cracking beak in a worm-eating world. In time, the detrimental characteristics will begin to disappear. Fitting into your environment ensures survival.

Competition and Cooperation

"I've seen enough of those *National Geographic* specials." Aunt Bernice piped in. "Survival of the fittest is more gory than a Martin Scorsese movie."

There is the tendency is to interpret "survival of the fittest" as a bloody competition for food, territory, or mates. But competition between individuals is only part of the bigger reality of environmental adaptation, a category that also includes weather and rude neighbors (predators and pests).[11]

Back to the corn and its pest for a second. If a random genetic change in corn manifests as pest-resistance, this change in the corn puts pressure on the pest to change too. The change in the corn does not *cause* a change in the pest, but it does bid an adaptive response. When drugs are created to fight bacteria, the expectation is that in time, unless the bacteria is wiped out, the bacteria will evolve to develop drug resistance. For the bacteria to thrive, it will have to change. For the pest to survive (and he wants to live as badly as the corn does), the pest will have to change too. We call this "selection pressure." As the corn-eating pest reproduces and its DNA mutates, the pressure is on to come up with a trait that gets him the corn. When that inevitably happens, the evolutionary ball is back in the corn's court. In this way the corn and its pest are said to "co-evolve." The change in one results in the adaptive response of the other.[12]

In addition to classic Darwinian competition for resources in order to survive, there are plenty of instances where organisms cooperate for evolutionary reasons. Organisms mutually help each other survive in a process called *symbiosis*. While DNA shows how all organisms are related (more on that later), symbiosis shows how everybody needs everybody else. The most important event in biological history was the production of the first multicellular organisms, which scientists propose happened as the result of the symbiosis between two ancient bacteria.[13] With symbiosis, organisms display complex patterns of interdependence.[14] They work together and depend on each other. Off the coast of Indonesia, a shrimp swims alongside a Gobi fish. As the shrimp labors to convert coral reef debris into edible victuals for them both, the Gobi keeps an eye out for the predatory scorpion fish that would otherwise feed on the working shrimp. There are crabs that clean sea cucumbers and in return get to take cover in the sea cucumber's bottom. A hummingbird and a flower in Mexico have this little dance going that guarantees one gets food and the other fertilization. This symbiotic cooperation is not intentional, however, but encoded in the genes of the organisms.[15]

Macro and Micro

So far Aunt Bernice had no serious objections. She likes flowers and hummingbirds. And she doesn't want bugs in her corn. "I understand breeding," she said. "I get cocker-poodles and labradoodles, but they're still all dogs. Just don't try telling me there are *corn*dogs, I mean, except the kind you eat on a stick."

The distinction she draws is a familiar one between microevolution (changes within species) and macroevolution (changes from one species to another). A lot of folks will say they believe in microevolution but just can't allow for the evolution from a fish to a dog (not that evolution ever operates that directly). These folks are right. There is no such thing as macroevolution. But there is such a thing as one species giving way to a new species. The qualitative change from one species to another is the accumulation of all the infinitesimal changes that preceded it. The reason that there is no macroevolution is because all evolution is micro. Any variations that occur in an individual happen at the genetic (micro) level. As some of these individual variations get selected (or lie dormant and are carried along until selected later) by nature, they get passed on and further modified by succeeding variations until the accrued changes render the species different enough that a new species results. The "macro" change is the final outcome of all the prior micro-changes.[16] Evolution does not take major leaps. Fish don't elbow themselves onto dry ground overnight and then turn into poodles. An immense number of micro-changes occurred over millions of generations through millions of years before a fish ever took on the name *mammal*. A fish had to become an air-breathing fish that became a crawling fish that became a lizard that became a warm-blooded lizard that became a warm-blooded mammal and on and on through incremental stages over eons of earth history. The process is fairly steady and continuous.[17]

Change Is A Good Thing

But again, the changes don't line up single file. Though it's legitimate to view the historical development of multicellular organisms to vertebrates to mammals to humans as progressive, the survivors survive at the expense of many that never make it. The fish with elbows is one of a bunch of elbowed fish, some of which adapt to land and others that stay with the backstroke. Some regress (due to dysfunctional variations) and some go extinct. It all depends on an organism's particular adaptability and environment. Out of six air-breathing fish, three might go on to develop necessary traits that allow them to elbow themselves onto land. Out of those three, through reproduction there might emerge thirty others that develop the ability to travel around on land, allowing them to stay longer. Eventually what you have is not really a fish at all, but something brand new (taxonomically speaking). Calling a fish living on land without gills a fish would be . . .

"Fishy. Which is what all of this is still sounding like to me," Aunt Bernice said, an eyebrow raised. She felt she'd been led too far down a road she had had no intention of traveling. No way this was going to fly in her mind now (or swim or crawl or whatever).

Tick Tock

"Charles Darwin himself admitted that his theory was a sham if there wasn't enough time allowed for it to work," I said. "In the nineteenth century, the jury was still out. No one yet imagined creation to be as old as physics and astronomy would show it to be. The hardest thing to accept about evolution is that the complexity we observe in nature could ever be the result of chance. Now you understand it's not merely chance, but chance and necessity through natural selection."

"I may understand it, but that don't mean I'm accepting it." Aunt Bernice has her own line in the sand. She also has to be able to explain herself to the United Methodist Women's Circle.

It *is* hard to accept that all the variation exhibited on earth ever could have surfaced randomly (even with natural selection). When you talk about getting from a fin to an elbow, you're talking about a change that would take an awfully long time to happen randomly, so long, in fact, that some think traditionally understood evolution can't account for it all. Moving from a fin to an elbow awaits the chance appearance of favorable mutations (and by waiting, sometimes we mean millions of years). But as it turns out, the slightest genetic modification can result in significant morphing of individuals. Also, the same genes and pathways are reused over and over again. Novel developments rely on what's already present, limiting the need for a brand-new mutation to occur every time.[18] Sex speeds things up significantly. Both sex and the conservation of prior favorable changes dramatically increase the number of variations from which natural selection can choose. Sex itself evolved as a means of improving evolution. Evolution crafts the very capacity of creatures to evolve. The more reproduction, the more genetic diversity and the better the possibility of hitting on an adaptive characteristic.[19] (By the way, this is another reason not to clone yourself. Cloning severely diminishes the gene pool.)[20]

Step One and Two

Variations in individuals over time (evolution step 1) along with natural selection of the best fit variations (step 2) can also account for the complexity of specific organs within organisms: eyes, wings, and brains, for instance. One question might be why didn't all organisms become similarly complex? If people come from fish, why is it that some fish just stayed fish? Why don't humans have wings? The answer is that evolution works primarily on individuals. There's selection pressure on corn in one climate to adapt and become pest-resistant whereas the same corn is under no such pressure in a climate without that particular pest. Some fish do fine as fish; some significantly benefited by evolving into mammals; and others were able to stay somewhere in between (get a load of the bizarro, duck-billed, egg-laying mammalian platypus swimming around Australia to see what I mean). The environment determined which organisms evolved which way.

You have to have both steps of the two-step process to have evolution. Without step 1, genetic variation (whether through mutation or reproduction), everybody would be identical twins and the gene pool stagnant. As soon as some dramatic environmental change occurred (an ice age, for instance), everybody would get wiped out because they couldn't adapt to the cold. With no diversity in the gene pool, no individuals could develop the necessary adaptive capabilities (fur and the ability to hibernate, for instance). Without step 2, natural selection ("survival of the fittest" through competition or cooperation), genetic mutation would yield chaos and extinction because most mutations are disadvantageous or harmful.[21] But working together, variation and selection have made possible the emergence of corn, worms, fish, ducks, dogs, and people—all from microscopic bacteria (which, again, continues to be the dominant organism on earth). Even though it is not a self-conscious process, evolution is remarkably creative.[22]

"If you wanted to get really creative, Aunt Bernice, you could say that the evolution two-step is akin to God's command that creation 'be fruitful and multiply' (Gen 1:22, 28). While on the surface *be fruitful* and *multiply* seem like synonymous terms, it's not so hard to imagine how being fruitful could correspond to genetic variation and multiplying could correspond to successful reproductive survival as a result of natural selection. You could say that evolution is in the Bible."

"Don't be sacrilegious," she said disapprovingly. There were days she had trouble believing I was a minister. "Don't try to make God into an evolutionist."

"I am trying to suggest that God and evolution may be connected. After all, if evolution actually did happen, then God would have had something to do with it."

She just shook her head and sighed. "I think somebody needs to read their Bible better."

Fossil Findings

Before we do that, let's go back for a deeper dig into the evidence. First the fossils. If you think of the history of nature as analogous to a crime scene, fossils are the physical evidence of what happened. We can't look into the past, but we can look at what the past left behind. Granted, the vast majority of living organisms leave nothing behind. It's not easy to become a fossil (which is why there are so many missing links in the fossil record). You have to die in just the right place at the right time. If you die on land, you need to die near an erupting volcano in order to get buried fast enough by the volcanic ash so as to avoid decomposition or having your carcass digested by predators. Better to die underwater so as to get buried by sediment since disruption to your body would be a little less likely.[23]

The scarcity of fossils makes their reliability suspect in some critics' minds. But even though they are scarce, all the fossils that have been found line up in the order, time, and place they're supposed to if evolution is an accurate depiction of reality.[24] For instance, the earliest fossilized reptiles are more amphibian-like than any fossilized reptiles that follow. The earliest mammals have reptile-like characteristics. The same with birds. They are so similar to another group of reptiles that some paleontologists have formally proposed that birds be classified as a subgroup of the dinosaurs.[25] In species after species, unearthed evidence directly links each to a similar species preceding it in geologic time.

Paleontologists (fossil hounds) presume that given the rarity of fossilization, there must be an exponentially greater number of specimens that existed than those for which we currently have fossils. Some fossils provide clear evidence of missing links (transitional forms), such as the fish with elbows in their fins. But paleontologists are looking for more than these transitional forms. For instance, whales and hippos are each other's closest living cousins. But because evolution isn't linear, we don't necessarily expect to find a whale-o-potamus anywhere on the family tree. Instead, what we expect to find some day (if indeed a fossil exists) is a common ancestor, now extinct, from which the whale and the hippopotamus each descended. Whenever organisms share similar characteristics (anatomical or genetic), it is because they share a common ancestor. You have to go backwards on the family tree to find the link; you can't swing from limb to limb. And when you do go backwards, you can't help but view a smooth continuity aptly explained by evolution.[26]

"So what about humans?" Aunt Bernice demanded to know. She didn't care so much about whales and hippos.

"Turns out that chimpanzees are our nearest relatives."[27] I told her. "Chimps are more closely related to humans than they are to gorillas."

She could believe that. "Sounds like your cousin Wyatt," she said.

If chimps and humans descended from common ancestors, fossil bones of these common ancestors should show up on our petrified family tree. And sure enough, they do—over and over again. Bunches of intermediate skeletal remnants have been found, especially skulls. The earliest fossils that are related to primates have been dated to around two million years ago in Africa, with hominid (humanlike) bones showing up in Europe around 250,000 years ago. The European skull fragments reveal modern-sized brains, though the tools (found alongside the skulls) used by these hominids had hardly advanced from tools used by previous smaller-brained generations. Clearly, brain size ain't all it's cracked up to be. In between the earlier, smaller skulls and the modern-sized ones are plenty of other intermediate skulls, each of which further confirms the existence of creatures that lived in the times between early primates and people, even though paleontologists aren't yet sure about who (or what) they were.[28]

DNA Evidence

But the fossil evidence, as persuasive as it is, hardly stacks up to the credibility of DNA evidence. The impact of genetics on evolution is as significant as it has been on crime scene forensics. The same extreme precision of genetic matching that has led to the overturning of unjust verdicts in rape and murder cases has shown a 98 percent match between chimpanzee and human DNA.[29] Our genes match up 50 percent with earthworms. Take a human gene, stick it into a monkey, a worm, or even a bacterium and it will likely work just fine. And vice versa (though you shouldn't try this at home). To argue that evolution worked to bring about animals and plants, but not people, is a bit of a stretch, genetically speaking. Through our genes, people relate organically to the rest of creation. Humans aren't that different from their world.[30]

Within the complexity of the genome, DNA, RNA,[31] and proteins work together to grow and divide cells into organs and organisms.

Because of the way DNA is organized (as a ladder with all the information required to copy itself located on each half ladder), replication is easy. DNA, RNA, and proteins basically work the same way in all living organisms, whether you're a bacteria, a broccoli, a baboon, or Aunt Bernice.[32]

"Do you want to get smacked?" she growled.

"It's just an alliteration," I said.

Take the DNA sequences (genomes) of bacteria, broccoli, baboons, and Aunt Bernice, run them all through a computer, and you'd be able to construct the entire tree of life based upon the similarities in the genomes alone (this has been done). Among the most surprising discoveries has been the old age of so many of the genes.[33] You can trace some of them all the way back to the first bacteria.[34] Moreover, evolution predicted that since most genetic mutations manifest no traits, we should see piles of obscure DNA lying all over our chromosomes. Up to this point, the accumulation of unused DNA was referred to as "junk DNA."

"God don't make no junk," Aunt Bernice snapped defiantly.

Actually, that's true. Even what's referred to as junk DNA is turning out to be more important than originally thought. For years the idea was that proteins did all the work of heredity, and that RNA (once thought to be DNA's lackey) only acted as an intermediate step between a gene and a protein. It now appears that some RNA may have a function all on its own, apart from translating a protein (talk about the last being first!). Anyway, from an evolutionary perspective, it didn't make sense for the genome to haul around junk that didn't do anything.[35] Now, instead of it being junk, it may be that the ambiguous mutations are savings in the bank, awaiting RNA execution and natural selection. Place these genetic discoveries alongside the fossils, throw in molecular biology (which shows the strong similarities of crucial substances like hemoglobin across species)[36] and comparative anatomy (people have four limbs as do lizards and birds, for example),[37] and the convincing scientific support for evolution (including the evolution of humans) is hard to ignore.

"It's not hard to ignore. *I* ignore it." Aunt Bernice shot back.

But that's the problem. By ignoring it, faith and science become so separate that faith no longer has anything to say about anything that's not subjective or supernatural. You avoid arguments you can't win while retiring to a "cozy warren of warm, fuzzy irrelevancy."[38]

"Better to be irrelevant than a baboon or a worm," Aunt Bernice replied.

Just because humans are genetically related to monkeys and worms hardly means that humans are indistinguishable from monkeys and worms. Genetically speaking, humans differ both in the amount and the distribution of gene diversity.[39] Data suggests it would have taken around seventeen hundred initial human individuals to achieve this diversity, which means either that early people were willing to travel halfway around the world to find a spouse or that the human population has until recently (geologically speaking) lived in a very small area.[40]

"Like the garden of Eden," Aunt Bernice smiled coyly.

"Right. Except I'm pretty sure there weren't seventeen hundred people in the garden of Eden."

Big Bang and the Bible

Though now that you bring up the Bible, the fact that God "created the heavens and the earth" (Gen 1:1) and commanded "the earth [to] bring forth living creatures of every kind" (1:24) could be interpreted to suggest the sort of interrelatedness toward which evolution points. This includes people too since we also read that "God formed man from the dust of the ground" (2:7). That the earth is the same as "the dust of the ground" implies that all things are comprised of the same material. The same elements that make up inorganic matter are present in organic matter too. Astrophysics traces the origins of these fundamental elements back to the birth of the stars. The "dust of the ground" was stardust before it was anything else. The elements that make up all matter were produced within astral "factories" located deep inside some ancient, first-generation star and then scattered throughout the universe by a supernova blast.[41] Ashes to ashes, stardust to stardust. As creatures we are related to all living things—to the plants and animals—but we are related to the minerals too. We are connected to the present but also, by a common legacy of physical events, to the past.[42] The carbon in our bodies ultimately traces back to a Big Bang.[43]

Astrophysicists postulate that the universe began with a blast of unimaginable proportions, a bang so intense and dense that out of it exploded everything that exists. Three major pieces of evidence point to a Big Bang.[44] The first is the way, according to something called "Hubble's red shift," that almost all the galaxies in the universe are moving away from our own.[45] Space itself is expanding everywhere and fast. It's blowing up like a big balloon that keeps inflating.[46] Deflate the balloon and you'd get back to a common exhalation (explosion) sometime around thirteen billion years ago. The second piece of evidence is what's called "cosmic microwave background radiation." The early, blistering universe spewed intense radiation. Yet as the universe expanded following this Big Bang, it cooled down. We can observe this cooling in the longer wavelengths of radiation coming at us from every corner of the sky (the longer the wavelength the cooler the radiation). Astronomers can rewind the radiation process back to its origins, again, somewhere around thirteen billion years ago. Finally, about a quarter of the ordinary matter in the universe is helium. This is much more helium than could have been produced by normal cosmological function, that is, had the universe had no explosive beginning. However, the conditions right after this Big Bang were optimal for the fusion of hydrogen (the prevalent element of the universe) into helium, thus accounting for the larger proportion of helium.[47]

"Thirteen billion years?!" Aunt Bernice was shocked. "What happened to six days?"

"Well, whatever Genesis meant by 'six days,' I don't think it meant six *literal* days."

Aunt Bernice's back stiffened.

If the universe had been created in six twenty-four-hour days, then the stars Adam saw on his first night of existence would have been just two days old, even though the light they emitted was still light years away. If God created the universe in six days, then he would have had to create all the intervening light so that Adam could enjoy a starry night.[48]

"God can do whatever he pleases," she sternly affirmed.

True, but why would it please God to make it look as if stars were as old as they are if in fact they weren't?[49] If "the heavens declare the glory of God" (Ps 19:1 NIV), shouldn't we expect the glory they declare to accord with what we actually observe and can measure? Otherwise God comes off as something of a con artist, fooling people into believing something that is untrue. And if God is a con artist . . .

"God cannot lie and still be God," Aunt Bernice said, opening her own Bible to Titus 1:2 ("God, who never lies").

"Yes ma'am," I agreed. "I'm counting on that."

That the universe expands suggests that it exists as a unified, vibrant entity. Albert Einstein's theory of special relativity showed that time and space operate as a singular entity we call space-time.[50] Space-time is now conceived as a dynamic quantity, an entity in and of itself (and a curved one at that). When something exists or moves in space, its presence affects the curvature of space and time, which in turn affects the movement of everything else.[51] Astrophysics therefore joins biology in demonstrating the interrelatedness of all things. Mass itself winds up being the same thing as energy, just in a different form (like steam and ice are both water in different forms). When one thing moves, something else gives. Everything has implications on everything else. The "heavens and the earth" are a matched set at both the beginning of time and at the end. The extremely ancient universe makes room for an ancient earth—some 4.5 billion years old. The age of the earth is calculated by measuring the ratio between three radioactive chemical elements present in rocks which steadily decay and transform into different, stable elements. Uranium slowly becomes lead, potassium slowly becomes argon, and the more exotic strontium becomes the rare element rubidium.[52] If the earth was created a few thousand years ago, then rocks and minerals everywhere would match, showing greater ratios of the radioactive elements to the stable elements. The proportion of uranium in any rock would be the same as in every other rock. But instead, over and over again, different ratios are found in older rocks than newer ones, indicating that the age of the earth actually approaches 4.5 billion years.[53] Enough time for evolution (variation with natural selection) to have occurred as theorized.

This Porridge Is Just Right

Science shows that the immensity of time was essential for the evolution of life. We now know that about eleven or so billion years are needed for the necessary ingredients of life to cook inside stars and then to disperse into a new generation of stars with planets like ours, conducive to starting and sustaining organic existence.[54] But even with such an immensity of time, the plausibility of life forming required very specific conditions. Had the universe not emerged exactly as it did, life would have never spawned. Now, it should be noted that one of the most problematic aspects of evolutionary theory has to do with the emergence of life from non-life. Ideas on how to explain this abound, though it's probably safe to say that for now, the onset of viability remains a scientific mystery.[55]

Aunt Bernice piped up, "*I* know how life started."

"I didn't say it was a *theological* mystery, Aunt Bernice."

As for what we do know, we know that the physics of the universe basically operates in accordance with four fundamental forces or interactions. These interactions consist of attractive and repulsive forces, decay, and annihilation. All existence depends upon these interactions. The four fundamental interactions include gravity (which affects objects of relatively large mass) and electromagnetism (the interaction between two charged particles which is what basically keeps you from plummeting through the floor as you read this). However, once you get down to the quantum level, gravity and electromagnetism for the most part give way to the "strong" nuclear force (which holds the nucleus of an atom together with force carrier particles called *gluons* because they so tightly glue quarks together to form nuclei; names such as *hold-on* and *duct-tape-it-on* were also considered)[56] and the "weak" nuclear force (which causes radioactive decay; it's responsible for the unstable matter of the universe becoming stable).

Each of these forces has to be just as it is for life to exist. If gravity's mathematical value had been just a bit stronger, the universe would have collapsed before life could have emerged; a little weaker, and the earth would never have formed. If electromagnetism were just a little stronger, electrons would be so tightly bound to atoms that the formation of chemical compounds would be impossible; a little weaker, and atoms would disintegrate at room temperature. If the strong nuclear force were a little weaker, no elements other than hydrogen would have formed following the Big Bang; just a little stronger, all of the hydrogen in the universe would have converted into helium (and we'd all talk funny). Without hydrogen there could be no sun, no stars, no water, no you, no me. The same sort of thing holds true for the weak nuclear force.[57] When unstable particles become stable, they're said to change "flavors." Without the flavor-change, the universe would have no taste. Nothing would matter because there would not be enough stable matter to form a universe.

Then there's the expansion rate of the universe. Renowned physicist Stephen Hawking observed that "if the rate of the expansion of the universe one second after the Big Bang had been smaller (or larger) by even one part in 100 thousand million, the universe would have collapsed (or been unable to form) before it ever reached its present size."[58] The expansion calculations, which make life possible, have also made cosmologists think that the universe should have slowed down more than it has by now—gravity being gravity. But recent discoveries are generating questions as to whether other weird energies are at work, energies currently labeled "dark energy," which is needed to account for the increasing expansion rate of the universe. There's also peculiar "dark matter" that is necessary for explaining the motion of galaxies. Dark matter is a bizarre kind of antigravity that, while infinitesimally small, turns out to be extremely strong (talk about a paradox!) and universally dispersed. As you might imagine, physics is a discipline best suited for insomniacs.[59]

Anthropic Principle

This knife-edged, precision-tuning of the universe's fundamental interactions (including the universe's specific rate of expansion) contributes to what is called the "anthropic principle" (*anthropic* from the Greek word for human). Basically, the anthropic principle states that the physical laws of the universe *must* be exactly as they are in order for human life to exist. If the fundamental interactions didn't occur exactly as they do, then we wouldn't be here to observe them occurring exactly as they do.

"Hmm, that sounds like one of those chicken-or-the-egg kind of problems," Aunt Bernice said. Aunt Bernice is quite bright.

And quite right. We observe physical laws to be necessary for human life because we humans are alive to observe the physical laws. A huge fuss is made over the anthropic principle given its religious implications. Physicists don't like having to fall back on an Almighty Knife Sharpener who honed everything cosmologically perfectly just prior and milliseconds after the Big Bang. Accounting for the anthropic principle does invite some metaphysical meddling, though believers should always be wary of basing their faith on questions science has yet to answer. To base the existence of God on the silences of science soon turns the Lord of creation into that "God of the gaps." Gap theology seeks to demonstrate God's existence by pointing to the absence of a scientific explanation. It's a bad strategy. Scientific advancement is committed to filling its holes in ways that faith cannot. While there's always a new scientific discovery, faith doesn't demand that God reveal himself in new ways, different from what we believe the Bible discloses. So far, each new piece of scientific data has fit the evolutionary puzzle (which is why Darwin's is such a good theory). For those who hold on to a God of the gaps, each fitting piece pokes another hole in their faith. Before long their God is full of holes himself.

Theorists have offered various suggestions to account for the compatibility of the universe with the existence of intelligent life. There's unbelievable luck (the odds of which are so infinitesimally small as to not be taken seriously) or multiple, parallel universes allowed by quantum theory. The idea is that given enough universes, you'll eventually hit on one capable of supporting life. There's also hope for a grand unified "theory of everything," that holy grail of physics bringing together the heretofore incongruent realities of gravity and quantum mechanics.[60] But at this point, the plausibility of unbelievable luck, multiple universes, or holy grail hope is no more plausible than faith in God. And even if there are multiple universes or a final theory, these discoveries still need not negate God's creative hand behind them.

"Well, praise the Lord for that," Aunt Bernice said, heaving a very relieved sigh.

The idea of fine-tuned forces doesn't *prove* God, but a fine-tuned universe does make more sense with a force behind the fine tuning. If you're a scientist who believes in God, there's no need to check your faith at the door of the physics lab. This also goes for the door of the biology lab, at least inasmuch as you're willing to admit that the emergence of something out of nothing defies adequate scientific explanation. How do you get from nonlife to life? Why is there something instead of nothing?

"I told you I know the answer to that one," Aunt Bernice stubbornly repeated.

"I know you do. Though you have to be careful that you're not staking your confidence too heavily on a dearth of competing hypotheses. Granted, science has no real stake in the existence of God; its concerns are primarily for what it can observe and measure. Yet for believers in God . . ."

"You still believe in God?"

"Yes, Aunt Bernice. For *we* who believe in God, the issue is not 'does science prove God?' but given what science reveals, 'what does science reveal about God?' In other words, if God is the maker of heaven and earth, as we believe, then what do the heavens and earth, as science describes them, have to say about God?"

Orderly Disorder

Scientists currently describe the universe in terms of two basic yet partial and seemingly contradictory theories: Albert Einstein's general theory of relativity and quantum theory.[61] General relativity lays out the universe as a collection of well-defined objects existing in a smooth (albeit curved) geometrical space-time.[62] It accounts for the movement of planets and galaxies and shows how large objects relate and affect each other. It's all very orderly and very predictable, once you understand the math (not that the math is easy to understand). However, once we descend into the microscopic realm, quantum theory rules over a random, haphazard house of mirrors where objects behave as both particles and waves, and where all that is certain is that nothing is certain. Quarks and leptons and gluons, in all sorts of flavors, charm and strange (physics terms) their ways up and down, all over the place, without any predictable rhyme or reason (quarks have quirks). Three of the four fundamental interactions of physics (electromagnetism and the strong and the weak nuclear forces) work on and with quantum particles according to what is called the standard model of particle physics (though "standard" is something of a stretch given the way that quantum theory functions). Despite all its capriciousness, the standard model works remarkably well. It has proven to be outstandingly productive and accurate in its mathematical predictions of particle behavior (usually down to the eleventh decimal place). I wouldn't be typing on this computer without it (because there would be no microprocessors). The only place where quantum theory fails is where gravity rules, namely, in the visible universe where you, me, and Aunt Bernice reside.[63] This baffling disconnect may have been what made Einstein's hair stick out like it did.[64]

This separation of powers between quantum theory and gravity drives ordered, unity-loving, paradox-hating physicists crazy. If everything in creation interacts with everything else, how can reality be governed by two contrasting and divergent theories? Biology allows that everything is related, but physics reminds us that relatedness is a long way from homogeneity. Large-scale matter obediently and reliably follows the laws of gravity, but subatomic matter at the quantum level does as it pleases. Uncertainty at the subatomic quantum level is inescapable. Unlike the mystery surrounding the origin of life or the anthropic principle (the precision-tuned laws of nature), there's no mystery to quantum indeterminacy. Unlike a planet in orbit or an apple falling from a tree, we know we don't know what a quark is going to do. And it's not because the instruments for measuring quantum behavior are faulty. On the contrary, the better the instruments and the measurements, the clearer the unpredictability. In accordance with the Heisenberg Uncertainty Principle (the closest thing to a law in quantum theory), any attempt to pinpoint a quark's behavior (its location and velocity simultaneously) is doomed.[65] Seek, but ye shall not find.

Ironically (or should I say paradoxically?), it's the indeterminacy of quarks that causes the universe to seem so determined and orderly. Although the behavior of an individual particle is totally unpredictable, throw a bunch of unpredictable particles together and the outcome of their collective behavior starts to make statistical sense.[66] It's like what happens when you throw a community hymn sing. The Baptists and the Episcopalians may go their own quarky ways most Sundays, but put a common hymnbook in their hands and you can get some sweet harmony (though don't ask me what in physics would serve as the hymnbook). It's because quarks play nice together that their particular particle whimsy doesn't lead to universal chaos.

However, quantum indeterminacy, inasmuch as it is foundational to all matter, does contribute to an open-ended reality for matter. The universe may be *orderly*, but that's not the same as saying it's *determined*. We know how the cosmos works, but we don't necessarily know where it's headed (scientifically speaking). This open-endedness is what is meant when scientists say that evolution is random. Random does not mean chaotic, but it does mean unpredictable. Quarks dart around inside the genome (and thus inside you) spurring genetic variation and mutation in unforeseeable fashion. Thus the *random* nature of nature itself. Variation in nature can turn on a subatomic, particle-sized dime.[67] Because of this random nature of nature, a second roll of the cosmic dice could easily turn up completely different.[68] It just happened to turn out the way it did this time.

"Are you trying to tell me that we're here by accident?"

No way Aunt Bernice was going to believe that. And who can blame her? Even though evolution has withstood some of the most strenuous empirical and theoretical scrutiny, almost nobody swallows it whole. It doesn't make intuitive sense. How can anything as beautiful and systematic as the world we inhabit and observe "just happen"? Some scientists postulate that the human brain is simply not wired to accept the reality of randomness. Just as we're not wired to see infrared light, our brains can't make sense of the apparent senselessness of evolution. It's as if we were "natural-born creationists"—naturally selected to propose a supernatural cause in the face of capriciousness and to attribute meaning and purpose even where there is none.[69] This evolved tendency to see meaning and purpose also affects how we see ourselves. We don't see ourselves as bodies, but rather as inhabited (or inspirited) bodies—this despite science showing that whatever we mean by soul or spirit includes the brain. You can't say "I believe" apart from your neurons firing in physical fashion. You can live with an artificial heart for a spell, but take away your brain and you're no longer you.

Of course this begs the question: how can someone be wired for creationism and still believe in evolution? An evolved brain is not a fixed machine; again, to have evolved is not to have been predetermined. Roll those dice a second time . . . We can say that genetic mutation and natural selection resulted in a brain with certain predilections (such as toward creationism), but the brain nevertheless *learns* in such a way that interacting with its environment shapes its future. Whether genes or learning is the more influential agent is the old nature-nurture debate.

But the debate sets up an unnecessary dichotomy. Both an organism's makeup and its environment play crucial roles in its development. This is true within evolution itself. Genetic variation (inherited traits) required natural selection (environmental interaction) for evolution to happen. Howeve, when we speak of the human brain, we're really talking about something that has out-evolved evolution. The human brain's capacity for learning makes it possible for people to control their future in ways that other animals cannot. We may be evolved to believe in God, but we don't have to.

"OK, honey. You've worn me out." Aunt Bernice rose stiffly from her red brocade, wingback chair. She moseyed off to bed with every intention of saying some serious prayers for me.

CHAPTER 3

WHAT HAPPENS WHEN I THINK TOO MUCH

The Who and Why of Creation

So much (for now) for the science. What about the theology? How have Christians for centuries understood the ways the world works?

Here's how I learned it:

"In the beginning God created the heavens and the earth" (Gen 1:1 NIV). This straightforward introductory declaration sets the stage for the rest of the Bible. God's role as the originator of everything gets announced up front. When it comes to visible reality, God made it. When it comes to invisible reality, God made that too. By his word and his will, he made everything that is, out of nothing that was, because there was nothing before God. God existed before existence itself. That God made everything "out of nothing" is so important that it gets its own Latin designation: *ex nihilo*. As Creator, God's work is first. No preexisting materials were required to do his job. No one advised him on it. The universe came to be by God's decision alone.[1] To be Creator is to be the sole Author of reality, the Reality who makes reality into reality. Or something like that.

"God said, 'Let there be light,' and there was light" (1:3 NIV). God said the word and it was so. Theology teaches me that as God is the Author of reality, whatever God speaks must be. "Let there be light" resulted in light. Why start with light? Why not? Light typifies God's pure existence (1 John 1:5). It enables sight and symbolizes goodness and truth. As light emanates from light, so creation emanates from God. But more than a fortuitous emanation, creation emerges deliberately. The Creator exists in eternal community as Father, Son, and Holy Spirit. As intrinsically *personal* and *relational*, God brings reality into being as an extension of his personality and relationality. Like light, God's love radiates out into the shape of a relational creation. But because God is love (1 John 4:16), he cares about his creation. He made the world to share in his community life as the trinitarian God.[2] This explains why loneliness feels so lonely.

God's authorship of reality also implies authority over reality. He's in charge (which is also what makes him God). Theology uses fancy words like *sovereignty* and *dominion* and *rule*, but the basic idea is that God's the Boss. He's not about simply getting the ball rolling "in the beginning" but keeping it rolling as he governs, guides, and sustains his creation, pulling it toward its appointed ends. God's ongoing involvement with his creation goes by another fancy theological word: *providence*. And providence itself breaks down into three kinds.

First there's ordinary providence, consisting of the laws of nature that God put in place to keep everything in order and to hold everything together (Col 1:16-17). Ordinary providence plays no favorites. Gravity pulls down on the just and unjust alike (Matt 5:45). Next there's extraordinary providence whereby God employs ordinary nature for exceptional purposes, like the way God used the wind to drive in enough quail for the Israelites to stuff themselves in the desert (Num 11:31). Extraordinary (extra-natural) providence demonstrates God's authority to do as he will with what he's made. It's the sort of thing actuaries label "acts of God," since no human can take responsibility for them. Finally you have supernatural providence (with the emphasis still on *natural* since miracles are entirely within God's nature to do). Supernatural providence (a.k.a. miracles), involve God suspending his own laws of nature for his own redemptive reasons (like with the resurrection of Jesus). Miracles also show up when God has a particularly irrefutable point to make (like with the plagues against ancient Egypt).[3] That miracles technically have God suspending his own laws sounds contradictory to critics (though we prefer to say *paradoxical*). But as Author of reality, God has authority to rewrite when he deems it necessary. (Nevertheless, miracles are by definition rare, even if they still fall within God's natural way of doing things. God does not suspend himself.)

As author of reality, God, like truth, exists as objective, freestanding reality, which means that he's not a figment of my imagination or a fabrication of my culture. Nobody made him up. God exists independent of my perception. Though I must have faith to know him, God does not need my faith to know me. As freestanding reality, God creates independently of his own free will and for his own reasons. Do we know these reasons? We can infer. The Bible doesn't really ask *how* God created, nor does it answer that question. *Who* and *why* matter most. From this *who* and *why*, a portrait emerges as to God's reasons for creating as he does.

As far as the *who*, theology teaches that God is not a metaphysical gambler. He does not randomly stake his creation on some fluky roll of the cosmic dice. Nor is God a distant deity, content to leave his world to fend for itself. God is not relegated only to those places where science is silent. The Lord may work in mysterious ways, but he also works in ways that science describes, ways that make perfect sense. God is not a hanger-on, dependent upon creation for his own identity. Creator and creation are not the same thing. For God to *make* the heavens and the earth means that the world is not a part of God but rather his production. Thus the cosmos, for all its immensity, is not sacred in and of itself. A clear distinction between Creator and creation is always upheld (as is the distinction between Creator and creatures).[5]

Above all, theology teaches that God is good (as in beautiful, beneficial, sensible, and right) and the creation he creates reflects this fundamental aspect of his character. Therefore theology declares that the world is good (Gen 1:31) because God is good. Wind, water, trees, toads, dandelions, and dirt—everything is good because a good God made it. God's imprint remains on creation, and thus creation retains its inherent goodness. Conversely, creation's inherent goodness—as revealed in its beauty, order, intricacy, and immensity—displays God's good hand (Job 12:7-9; Ps 19:1).

The only thing that God made that wasn't good was a *solitary* Adam (Gen 2:18). You can't have anybody being alone in a relational creation and call it good. Not even God is alone. As Trinity, God himself operates as an interpersonal God, or better yet, God is a *tri-personal* God (the logic of which squarely fits under the category of *mystery*). Therefore, "to make man in his image" meant God had to make interpersonal people. But since Adam was the creature, the Creator needed to make man in the plural. God said, "Let us make people in *our* image" (1:26 NLT, italics mine), employing the first person plural to underscore his own plural personality.[6] And so "God created humankind in his image, in the image of God he created them; male and female he created them" (1:27). God wired us for relationship and then made relationships possible.

As "made in the image of God," people are that part of creation who most resemble God (we're talking *ideally* here). Of all the creatures, humans love and speak in ways that look like the ways God loves and communicates (again, the emphasis is on *ideally*). Our relational and communicative traits that distinguish us from all other animals designate us to be caretakers of the creation. The Author bestows upon people some of his own authority to use for the good of the world (1:26). The Bible uses the word *dominion*, but *domination* was never in view. The idea was that a good God made good people to take care of the world. Our dignity and worth as people derives from our identity as God's creatures made to be like him. It's what makes us human.

But it's also what makes us foolish. "The woman . . . took of its fruit and ate; and she also gave some to her husband, who was with her, and he ate" (3:6). As a good God with free will, God gave his people free will to use for good. But we all know how that worked out. Our freedom was what led to our downfall; and, by extension (since everything is related), we brought the rest of creation down with us. It is our fault that the world's in the mess that it's in. So why did God endow people with authority *and* freedom if that meant giving them the power to screw everything up? It goes back to God's relational character. For God to enjoy relationship with his people implies that the relationship cannot be forced. A forced relationship is not a relationship of love. Love, by definition, is freely given and received, which means freedom to *reject* love on earth has to be a possibility.[7] A person is not truly free if he or she is not free to choose *wrongly*. Thus God allows for our freedom in order to have a genuine (and not a contrived) relationship with us.[8]

Now, the good news is that God is more devoted to this relationship than we are, so much more that he eventually shows up *in person* to redeem all our bad choices. God shows up in Christ (and not as a stone or a star or an animal[9]) to woo us and to win us back from the dark places in which our bad choices have trapped us. For us Christians, this is what makes the creation account complete. God makes the world, we mess it up, but God loves us too much to leave us in our mess. God guarantees a new start and a new creation for both ourselves and our world (2 Cor 5:17; Rev 21:1). He comes to us in Christ and not only redeems the mess (through his dying and rising from the dead) but redeems our freedom too. Indeed, the hallmark and pattern of true human freedom is Christ's own freedom, a human freedom that announces "not my will, but yours be done" (Luke 22:42 NIV). Human freedom, then, in its truest and best sense is always "freedom-for-God rather than freedom-against-God."[10]

The How of Creation

Note that in none of this is anything said about whether God created the world in six actual days or intervened with miracles when some species needed a boost. Again, the *who* and the *why* matter more than the *how*. Not that the *how* never gets mentioned. The words *six* and *days* appear in print. But you have to be careful or you'll get stuck trying to explain why God would bring forth vegetation and fruit (day 3) before putting in a sun or the seasons (day 4). Theology consistently stresses a crucial distinction between what the Bible *says* and what the Bible *means*. Not that the two aren't related; it's just that words are never so simplistic as to always be taken at face value. For example, the Hebrew word *day* (*yom*) can refer to the specific twenty-four-hour kind, but it also can refer to a longer period of time ("the day of their calamity" in Deut 32:35, or "the day of the Lord" throughout the Old Testament).[11] The usage corresponds to the way we use a word like *season* to mean either the exact length of time between equinox and solstice or a more general period of time during which factors continue on a common pattern ("baseball season"). The key to knowing the difference is understanding how the word works in the sentences and paragraphs where it appears. Sometimes this is obvious, other times not so. We're still debating what exactly Jesus *meant* when he said "my flesh is true food and my blood is true drink" (John 6:55), even though we know what all the words *say*.

Similarly with the Genesis account. The Bible says "six days," but there's no way that's right unless astrophysics and geology are patently false. God would have had to make the world with a made-up history, a false impression that would seem to fall outside the bounds of God's truthful nature (Num 23:19; 1 Cor 14:33). Why would God intentionally mislead us? To believe that "all truth is God's truth," means we also believe that correctly interpreted scientific discovery will always agree with correctly interpreted Scripture[12] and vice versa. OK, so the onus falls on the loaded caveat "correctly interpreted," but the point is that God is *consistent*. What he speaks in the Bible squares with what he shows us in nature.

But what if you interpret Scripture correctly only to have science say that you still have it wrong? Well, you could say that science has it wrong. And science may have it wrong. This has been the crux of the debate between Christianity and evolution. Given what we know the Bible to *say*, has not science clearly deciphered nature wrongly? The problem here is that scientific methods tend toward a precision that theological methods cannot attain. Not that scientists are *never* wrong; it's just that scientific misinterpretation usually can't last very long. Due to science's rigorous scrutiny, experiment, and replication, mistakes eventually yield to the facts. That's why we call them "scientific facts." You can say "I don't believe the facts," but that doesn't make them any less true in their representation of the way things are. You can say "evolution is just a theory," but that doesn't make it any less accurate in its description of the way life on earth works. Besides, scientific theories are not like hunches or even educated guesses. Scientific theories must not only describe the world correctly, they must also guide scientific research dependably. Theories make it possible to trust medicines to do what they do. Scientific theories are why we can type on computers and drive our cars and check weather forecasts (if not rely on them).

The scientific evidence is too strong in evolution's favor to reasonably deny its occurrence. You can refuse to believe it, but that still won't make it untrue, any more than denying God exists proves that he doesn't exist. The overwhelming evidence in favor of evolution has led plenty a Christian to suggest that the Bible tells the *who* and the *why* of creation (the prime or final cause), leaving evolution to describe the *how* (the secondary or efficient cause). And that works as long as you don't think about it too much. This is my problem. I think too much. Theology teaches me that the character of creation reflects the character of the Creator—God's beauty and order and goodness and purposefulness. But as soon as you start thinking about what an evolving creation truly reveals—namely, cruelty and disorder and indifference and randomness—you can't help but wonder about your faith and about the God to whom that faith points.

Laws of Creation

When Darwin first proposed evolution, you could still look at the world through a theological lens and recognize the part God had to play.[13] Even as natural selection picked which species made the grade, something (someone?) had to tweak the variations in the individual creatures on which natural selection would operate. Who did it? God did it! How else would you explain the ways that offspring differed from their parents? That stuff doesn't just happen! But once James Watson and Francis Crick figured out the double helix structure of deoxyribonucleic acid (DNA) in 1953, suddenly you could say variation *did* "just happen." Any reliance by biology on theology to explain heredity became unwarranted. The "modern synthesis" between Darwinism and genetics (what some people call "Neo-Darwinism") confirmed suspicions that DNA carried life's transmissible information. Some folks started wondering what was there left for God to do.

There's still ordinary providence. Christians believe God wrote the laws that evolution abides by. All that fine-tuning of the earth's fundamental forces, which make life possible—somebody had to do that. And what about the Big Bang? Astrophysics can explain everything that happened after the Bang, but what about everything that happened before? Somebody had to light the fuse. But given all the systematic and lawabiding behavior physics and biology display post-Bang, who's to say there weren't natural laws governing what happened before it too?[14] Why not just say that the physical constants exist on their own?[15] You can see the futility that comes with basing your belief in God on a lack of evidence in science. Basing your faith on scientific deficiency is like building a house on eroding sand (to borrow a metaphor; Matt 7:26). Eventually the house crumbles under the rising waters of scientific discovery.

Faith

Now, I happen to think this crumbling is a good thing. Basing your faith on the power of scientific evidence is great when science holds afloat what you already believe. But science brings its own set of problems too. Look at the majesty of a glorious mountain range at sunset or the incredible complexity of the human body, and it's easy to deduce the handiwork of God. But take off faith's rose-colored glasses and science forces you to dig underneath the veneer of majesty and incredulity to see the tortuous (as well as torturous) road down which mountains and bodies had to progress. Evolution hardly looks providential. The observable factors of evolutionary reality—the capriciousness of genetic mutation, the harsh impersonality of natural selection, and the carelessness of immense cosmic time—how can these be the evidence of a personal God's good and loving touch?[16] If the world was created by a good God as good, then you can't help but wonder whether *good* means something quite different from what the word *good* says.[17]

According to evolution, genetic variation occurs according to no particular plan. There's no discernable pattern. The millions of copies that DNA makes of itself inevitably result in an error (mutation) here or there, but there's no way of knowing when or where on the genome these errors will happen or which ones will translate into actual traits. OK, so here's something God knows. But if God knows, then why do so many mutations either end up on the trash heap or threatening an organism's survival? Mutations can be just as dangerous as they are helpful. If God knows, then what does he know? Science suggests that the variability of genes is due to the variability inherent at the molecular level. Randomness is the way of the quantum world. Quarks (that make up protons and neutrons to form nuclei, and then add electrons to make up atoms that make up molecules that make up genes) move this way and that with absolute unpredictability. Because we *know* that particle behavior is by definition indeterminate, the randomness of genetic mutation is not one of those currently unfilled gaps of science. Indeterminacy exists as characteristic of reality itself.[18]

The Will(y-Nilly) of God

Before scientific discovery of the quantum world, nature was thought to operate solely in accordance with Isaac Newton's laws and gravity. You knew that if you dropped a rock from your hand it would always fall toward the ground. And this is still true as far as rocks and other large objects are concerned. But shrink down inside those rocks (and everything else) and you find a nanoscopic world where nothing is for sure except that nothing is for sure. Gravity is present but has no effect. The deterministic laws of nature turn out to be based on quantum laws of (im)probability. Now, this doesn't mean that one day a rock dropped from your hand will float in the air. The probabilities of quantum theory tend to average out as you get to the big stuff. But it does seem to mean that uncertainty is all that is certain.

Is God no longer dependable? Or does this mean that God doesn't care? Quarks dart and genes mutate wherever they will without any apparent divine concern. What about God's intentionality and purposes? I guess we could say that the randomness of genetic variation is random on purpose, but at that point why not just go ahead and say *random?* We could say that God's ways don't make sense because his ways are not our ways (Isa 55:9). But what good is that if his ways come off as less competent and more haphazard than either human ideals or practice? We could say that the Creator is not the creature that he should act as humans would presume him to act (Num 23:19), that God's purposes accord with his own counsel and his own will (Eph 1:11). We could label it a mystery and a paradox and trust that the ends will makes sense of the means. But why would God choose such patently purposeless means to achieve his purposeful ends?

Purposeful Ends

And what *about* those purposeful ends? Evolution throws up evidence of billions of years of waste and futility. Sure, things turn out intelligently in the end (so far), but the road to get here apparently lacks any discernable rationale. No trait ever develops in an organism in response to an organism's need. Animals in cold climates didn't develop warm coats to offset the weather; they just died off until some trait showed up accidentally that was able to hack the snow. Observe the development from bacteria to Aunt Bernice and you marvel at what looks like evolution's ongoing improvement. But get out the map and you see that the apparent improvement was basically a series of lucky wrong turns.[19] Species that make it (and most don't) do so only by fluke. More often than not, survivors are those who happened to be in the right place at the right time. Creation, for all of its beauty and order, fought tooth and claw. There's no rhyme or reason. Maybe this is the miracle: that creation succeeded despite the haywire of life. But creation by evolution doesn't require miracles as long as it has enough time.

There's plenty of time: thirteen billion years, give or take. Such an amount of time is truly incomprehensible. Condense it down to a year with the Big Bang kicking off January 1, and the earth doesn't even show up until some time in September. The space between "in the beginning" and "earth" in Gen 1:1 comprises something like eleven billion years. Life on earth shows up about September 15, followed by multicellular organisms bumping around for the next month or so. You've got a burst of organisms on the scene after that (the so-called "Cambrian explosion"[20]), with the dinosaurs coming and going around Christmas. Mammals start to expand shortly thereafter (once there aren't any dinosaurs to eat them), with humans popping up so late on New Year's Eve that there's barely enough time to pucker up for a kiss. In evolutionary terms, your own life on earth isn't even a blink of an eye.[21] Supposedly the epitome of creation made in God's image, evolution makes us out to be more of an afterthought, if we're even a thought at all.

Mirroring Heaven

This is especially true when you consider the place in the universe where God chose to put his people. If you're going to make a garden of Eden that's supposed to resemble heaven, why stick it onto some tiny blip of a planet spinning around a below-average star, parked out on the periphery of a "nondescript galaxy dwarfed by thousands of others larger and more magnificent than our own"?[22] What kind of "very good" plan is that? Christians wave JOHN 3:16 signs ("God so loved the world that he gave his only Son" to save it), but why bother saving this planet? With such an immeasurably massive universe with which to work, why not just start over someplace else? There's practically an infinite number of planets to choose from. And if not this universe, pick another. String theory[23] suggests that the math of gravity and quantum mechanics can cohesively compute if there are multiple universes in existence.

Evolution not only takes place in an enormous universe (or universes), but it involves an enormous amount of death. The missteps and roadkill of evolution represent millions of years of organism expiration. Natural selection killed off most of the plants and animals in order to get to the ones we humans enjoy (and destroy). Not only was the dying off rampant, it's mandatory. The emergence of life depends on the death of prior life, generations of mutational and reproductive failure in order to come up with successful combinations. Moreover, Darwin's familiar struggle for survival—whether for resources or mates or against the elements—reveals a process in which cruelty and suffering are standard fare. Darwin wrote,

> We behold the face of nature bright with gladness, we often see a super-abundance of food; we do not see, or we forget, that the birds which are idly singing round us mostly live on insects or seeds, and are thus constantly destroying life; or we forget how largely these songsters, or their eggs, or their nestlings are destroyed by birds and beasts of prey we do not always bear in mind, that though food may be now superabundant, it is not so at all seasons of each recurring year.[24]

Love

Where's the love? Natural selection has no compassion. All it cares about is utility. If something doesn't work, it's done. Why would a personal and relational God resort to such an impersonal (and depersonalizing) process? Forget about a good God, evolution doesn't even allow for a *merciful* God. The best you get out of evolution is an *indifferent* God with little by way of recognizable compassion. This is not the kind of God you want hearing your prayers. This is not the kind of God who has a wonderful plan for your life. This is not the kind of God who is best defined as love and light. In fact, evolution contains so much dysfunction, so much excess and error in its processes, that to attribute evolution to any superior, intelligent, and benevolent Being is practically an insult.[25] If God is good, how can evolution be his way?

You could chalk all of this up (theologically speaking) to a "fallen creation." Blame it on the humans. Sin is one theological construct that holds up to scientific scrutiny.[26] There's no doubt humans are responsible for much of the current wrecking of earth—be it global warming, water pollution, deforestation of the rain forests, recent animal extinction, or suburban sprawl. Not to mention the mess we've yet to make for succeeding generations now that we've taken to manipulating genes. Tweaking a gene in an individual person or plant is one thing. Passing that tweak on with no idea of the consequences is something else (which is what makes the advances in genetic technology so problematic).

But you can't blame sin for the death that evolution causes. The vast amount of dysfunction, excess, and deviancy in the evolutionary process happened before people ever arrived on the scene. According to evolution, it's the vast amount of dysfunction, excess, and deviancy in the evolutionary process that *brought* people onto the scene. What does it mean to be "made in the image of God" if the manner of my making has been so chaotic and ungodly? Perhaps this helps explain our downfall, but how can you fall if you're already down?

Image of God

Theology teaches that God made the first humans out of dirt (Gen 2:7). God gave Adam the tasks of tending the garden and naming the animals (2:15, 19). We exhibit our distinct relation to God through our own creativity and care of creation. Apparently Adam's responsibilities date him around the time of the Neolithic, about 10,000 years ago.[27] However, fossil evidence indicates that humans show up long before that.[28] DNA traces human beginnings to around 100,000 years ago. But dating humanity's start isn't the insurmountable problem. Again, a day doesn't have to be literally *one day* and biblical genealogies (from which the date of the first humans might be biblically calculated) are known to emphasize one ancestor to the exclusion of another. Their purpose was to authenticate specific characters in the bloodline, not account for every individual.

Still, despite the Bible's de-emphasis on the *how*, the *how* has been the rub when it comes to the first people. It may very well be that God made Adam in a moment's time, out of the mud of the earth, and then Eve from a rib in his side. But genetically speaking, making Adam out of the mud means God also had to make Adam with a built-in genetic profile that pegged him (and Eve) to evolution's hominid branch.[29] DNA evidence indicates a population history for humans of more than merely two people.[30] We could argue that just as Adam (presumably) was created with age,[31] so Adam was created with genetic characteristics to make him look *as if* he were a natural part of evolutionary history—in accord with he evidence. But if you're going to say that God made Adam to look as if he evolved on purpose, then you might as well go ahead and say Adam evolved. Again, why would God intentionally mislead? If God creates as a reflection of himself but has to fake it to do it, what's to keep us from thinking we believe in a fake God?

See what happens when you think too much?

Religion Is for Dummies?

On the other hand, there are those who look at the scientific data and are convinced we Christians don't think enough. We've clearly placed our brains and our eyes in the offering plates at church. Darwinism provides everything necessary to explain biological reality. If we insist on holding onto faith, can't we see that the God such faith requires would be a God not worth believing in? Why insist on projecting meaning and purpose where none evidently exists? While there is plenty that remains unimaginably improbable to human understanding, appealing to something just as improbable as God to explain improbability makes no sense.

Since science can be read to exclude, or nearly exclude, the necessity of God, why do we bother believing? Why embrace the comforting thought of a benevolent Shepherd if it's based on false comfort? Why hold onto a divine plan for your life if evolution plainly shows that it's all up for grabs? Where does such faith in faith come from, anyway?

Some argue that faith is a function of brain development. We're wired to believe like we believe because it served our ancestors well. Faith is an evolutionary product that promotes survival by promoting risk. If you're convinced you're going to heaven after you die, you might be willing to take chances other organisms forgo. Faith also congeals identity within social groups, conferring greater strength for survival than would be available if life were every man for himself.[32] Faith is no more than another biological trait on which natural selection has operated.

I still believe that "all truth is God's truth," therefore I have to believe that my faith and science can coincide. Scientific findings and Scripture can be read together. Not that scientists' interpretations of science always agree with the Bible; that's obviously not the case. But people of faith

should be able to look at accurate descriptions of the world and see bib
lically congruent portrayals of God. So what happens when accurate
descriptions of creation don't look like the Creator about whom theol
ogy teaches? What if science is right? If the *who* of creation does matter
most, who is God now?

CHAPTER 4

E-HARMONY

B efore launching into a who-is-God-*now* answer, I should probably think a little about how I think about these things. How do faith and science integrate? Or better, how do I integrate them in my thinking? How do I get to the *who* through the *what is* that science reveals? And why is this important, anyway?

Denial

This is what my friend Dave wanted to know. I described to him my dilemma over the disconnect between evolution and Christian theology and he responded, "Who cares?" (Dave's a worrier. He knows that if he starts to care about this stuff he might have to ramp up his sleep medication.)

"You mean besides me?" I replied.

"No offense," Dave said, knowing that I think too much, "but why does it matter to my faith if evolution is true? I believe what I believe. I know God exists, and I know God is bigger than anything science asserts. Just because science can explain something doesn't make it so."

I guess you could say that. (Dave did.) But science is pretty tough to simply ignore. Its findings and effects factor into just about every practicality of life. Science carries the weight it does because its concepts bear such close relation to the actual reality we inhabit.[1] Science provides a systematic and reliable basis for understanding what is really going on in the natural world in ways that theology and its methods are not set up to do.[2] Clearly you don't *have* to care about the disconnect between faith and science (Dave was right about that). But just because you don't care about it or believe in it doesn't make science inconsequential (any more than refusing to believe in God renders him nonexistent).

Nevertheless, denial is one way many deal with the dissonance that evolution causes. Since the apparently random indifference of evolution can throw a wrench in anybody's theology, simply disregarding it at least reduces any angst. Besides, evolution doesn't noticeably affect everyday life (as long as you don't get sick and need medicine). People can go to school and do fine (as long as they avoid biology class). They can raise their kids without ever having to worry about whether humans evolved or were specially created by God (as long as the kids are homeschooled). People can go to church and never fret over fossils or DNA (depending on the church). As a matter of fact, denying evolution can help you feel better about yourself. Being expressly made by God gives us a sense of special purpose in the world. We can believe we were made for a reason and that each of us is unique.

Not that evolution repudiates uniqueness. Actually, evolution requires it. Natural selection depends on variation, which means it depends on individuals being different from one another. Take away the variation and species invariably become extinct. But that's not the same as saying God made you or me special. Or is it?

Either way, denying evolution to help us feel better about ourselves (or about God), isn't a good idea, especially if evolution is real. While Christianity is grounded in supernatural events that defy scientific explanation (like the incarnation and resurrection of Jesus), Christianity is also grounded in regular occurrences that science describes (such as nature's relationality, creativity, and elegance). Therefore, inasmuch as evolution adequately describes the regular occurrences of nature, to deny evolution is potentially to deny God's own creative craftsmanship. If evolution is true at all, then it has to be the way God operates in the world. If "all truth is God's truth," propping up the old divider between science and faith starts to look sort of silly. It's dissatisfying too. That's because when you get right down to it, the *how* of science and the *why* of faith aren't so completely different.[3] To describe the *how* of something begs speculation as to the *why*, and vice versa. Even randomness can have its reasons.

Still, to think about faith and evolution without walls between them is a daunting endeavor. For the science-minded, a move toward the faith side feels like an abdication of sanity. For them, too much of Christianity comes off as way too irrational to give it any serious consideration. For the faithful, ceding too much to science jeopardizes one's beliefs. Sure, accommodating Copernicus, Galileo, and Newton worked out fine (as it turned out, the earth does revolve around the sun); but letting Darwin into that circle is only asking for trouble. Let evolution describe the ways of God and you'll soon have God himself evolving. (We call this *process theology*; it fits with evolution but gives up an awful lot of orthodoxy to do so.) Best to maintain the divider. Keep faith and evolution separate—the same way we separate faith and money, faith and work, or faith and sex. No contact means no conflict. Blessed are the peacekeepers. Peace is a virtue.

Of course, honesty and integrity are virtuous too. To dodge issues that conflict with faith ironically betrays a lack of faith; it presumes you don't believe that what you believe can withstand scrutiny. But if we want faith to matter beyond our own personal devotion, we need it to converse with the way things actually are and not merely with how we want things to be. Again, if all truth is God's truth, then any search for truth leads to God no matter where you start. Faith can face facts without fear.

"Nice alliteration," Dave said.

Facing Facts

However, facing the facts does not mean fiddling with the facts to get them to support what you already believe. Sometimes beliefs may need to adjust. To insist that evolution is "just a theory" only minimizes evolution's enormous impact for good in areas such as biological and medical research and may miss the opportunity to acknowledge the wonder of God for the ordinary ways he works. At the same time, the goal of an honest conversation between science and faith is not to make faith scientifically palatable. Believing is not always seeing. We still "walk by faith, not by sight" (2 Cor 5:7). Science will dispute faith's certainty that purpose is wired into creation because science sees no tangible evidence for it. But faith must challenge science's certainty that such purpose is impossible.[4] Some scientists will cite evolution as proof that God does not exist. Faith must challenge scientific arrogance, which presumes that accurate descriptions of nature sum up everything there is to know and say about nature.

"You need to take a breath." Dave could see I was getting a little too passionate.

Evolutionary theory itself has no stake in the existence of God, despite some scientists' insistence on interpreting the data that way. *Deta* and scientists' *interpretations* of scientific data are not the same thing. Unlike confirmed data itself, interpretations of the data differ according to who's doing the interpreting. What the believer sees as the creative hand of God, the nonbeliever may view as a fortunate fluke, but both are still looking at the same thing. Reliable data is not a threat to faith. On the contrary, the better the data, the more credible our theological interpretations of it ought to be. And the more credible our theological interpretations of nature, the more credible is our witness to God as the competent creator of it.

"So what about miracles?" Dave's worries can sometimes fuel a certain provocativeness.

To affirm the competence of God's creation is not to discount miracles. Again, miracles are entirely natural for God, even if they are rare. Miracles, when they occur, are means of divine revelation. They're holy exclamation points. For God to disrupt his regular and competent mode of operation can only mean that he has something *really important* to communicate. Yet to depend upon them as proof of God's involvement is to suggest that God only operates outside the nature of his creation.

"OK, so far, so good. Applying theological reasoning to science can benefit faith. But try turning it around so scientific reasoning benefits theology." Dave knew that any quid pro quo would be a no-no. Apply scientific reasoning to faith and you may lose your faith.

Science doesn't put a whole lot of stock in things you can't test. Scientific thinking begins with a hypothesis (in this case a belief) and then checks it against the data (the observable and the measurable). If the data doesn't fit the beliefs, you either have to discount, dismiss, and explain the data away (that denial thing), or you've got to modify your beliefs.

Reductionism

Nevertheless, while it's better to adjust your faith than to fudge the facts to fit what you want to believe, this is only the case as long as "the facts" are in fact the facts. Scientific methodology is devoted to verifiable truth, but sometimes the method misleads. What science thinks is true in one generation can change (we call these changes "discoveries," or even "revolutions" or "paradigm shifts," and sometimes "mistakes"). Scientific logic acts reductively, striving to understand reality by reducing observed data down to its simplest components—atoms, genes, particles, and theoretical strings. Science isolates variables in order to set up controls and tests. But isolated variables don't tell the whole story. For instance, neuroscience postulates that human experience can be broken down into recognizable neural patterns; experience is what occurs between your ears. But is human experience *nothing but* thought? And is thought *nothing but* brain function? And is brain function *nothing but* neural patterns? And are neural patterns *nothing but* individual neurons firing in sequence? (Reductionism is sometimes referred to as "nothing buttery.")

"I like butter." Dave was getting peckish. He likes snacks.

So then take an example from nutrition. For the most part nutritional science involves studying isolated nutrients one at a time. But nutrients exist within the context of food, food within the context of diet, diet within the context of lifestyle, lifestyle within the context of culture, and culture within the context of geography.[5] Even the simplest food is a "hopelessly complex thing to study, a virtual wilderness of chemical compounds, many of which exist in complex and dynamic relation to one another, and all of which together are in the process of changing from one state to another."[6] This is why vitamins are sorry substitutes for meals. But if you're a scientist wanting to study food, the scientific method behooves you to reduce victual complexity down to its ingredients, even though a piece of fruit is clearly much more than the sum of its component nutrients. You can't ignore the complexities and contexts that contribute to making the parts do what they do together. It takes two to tango (and innumerably more to mango).

Don't get me wrong, scientific reductionism is undeniably powerful, but it can get off track. And if it can get off track with regard to food and human eaters, how much more so with regard to faith and human believers? To reduce human belief down to neurological parts ignores the complexities and contexts that contribute to making the parts do what they do together. Neurons fire in the context of intricate patterns that generate thoughts and emotions, which occur in response to events and perceptions. The brain itself responds physiologically to learning (akin to the way muscles respond to exercise). Personality predisposition plays a role, as do familial and personal relationships, cultural affiliations, and even the weather (try thinking clearly when you're sweltering). Reductionism is a valuable tool, but it is not sufficient to explain all facets of reality. It appears that even subatomic particles, the most reduced of the reducible, cannot properly be treated in a reductionist manner. Quarks themselves are subject to environmental disturbances that cause changes with ramifications that carry all the way up the ladder.[7]

Human Experience

Human experience, while an object of scientific study, is also a variable that affects scientific study. Take kinetic energy. The connection between mercury moving up and down in a thermometer and a concept we've named *kinetic energy* isn't based upon anything we can see but rather on our *experience* of the connection between the visible sign (mercury moving) and the energy it represents.[8] To call kinetic energy "just your experience." goes against the math (kinetic energy is one half the mass of the body times the square of its speed) that validates our experience of it every time. Sidestep over to Christian experience; writing off faith as "just your experience" should be done with similar hesitation. Let's say that someone asks, "Why are you so content?" The Christian responds, "I am content because of Christ who strengthens me" (see Phil 4:11-13). The link between contentment and Christ is not based on what we can see, but on the *experience* of the association between the visible sign (contentment) and the spiritual presence it implies. Faith relies on experience in similar ways that science does.

"Hang on just a minute." Dave has an objection. "Contentment could be as much a product of your successful self-delusion as of the Holy Spirit. The scientist's experience is upheld by reliable instrumentation that works the same every time. Not so with faith—sometimes there's contentment, and sometimes you might be faking it."

He makes a good point. Dave's notion of contentment might not be the same as mine. Dave's most content while hiking in the woods. For me it's being out on my bicycle.

It is the case that there are no reliable instruments (or mathematics) to measure contentment; but people still know contentment when they see it. Your particular experience of contentment may be suspect by itself, but not if it correlates with humanity's vast accumulated history of collective experience. None of this dismisses scientific methodology. It merely reminds us that science has limits, just as faith has its limits. It also reminds us that science relies on observation and human experience in ways that faith does too. There are other parallels. Both science and faith look to one-of-a-kind, unrepeatable revelations or singularities on which to develop hypotheses and establish doctrine.[9] Just as Moses' crossing of the Red Sea and the resurrection of Jesus substantiate Christian faith, so evidence of a Big Bang undergirds contemporary cosmology and the fossil record backs up evolutionary biology. (Of course, the Red Sea crossing and the Resurrection are *supernatural* events, while the Big Bang and evolution, as far as science knows, are natural events. Science does not yet know what caused the Big Bang or exactly how life first emerged from nonlife.) Finally, science and faith hold certain *a priori* positions. Even to begin scientific exploration, a scientist must be committed already to fundamental beliefs such as "the universe is intelligible" or "truth is worth seeking."[10] Similarly, the theologian begins with the fundamental belief that "God exists." None of this is to say that science and theology are the same; they're just not as dissimilar as we normally suppose.

Science does have the distinct advantage of speaking a more universal language. Its systematic methods operate as close to being independent of culture, race, and gender as anything we have going.[11] A Buddhist biologist and a Christian chemist will always agree about the properties of amino acid despite their disagreements over the state of the soul (or politics or the best restaurant, for that matter). This unifying character of scientific language should make science increasingly attractive to Christians. Christians believe in a God who shows no partiality (Deut 10:17) and in whom "there is neither Jew nor Greek, slave nor free, male nor female, for you are all one in Christ Jesus" (Gal 3:28 NIV). Gravity and the properties of light treat everybody the same. That scientific language speaks with a common voice regarding the nature of the universe can only strengthen theology's attempts at doing likewise.

"I got it. Science can be helpful to theology." See, Dave does care. I knew he did.

Interpretation

A fruitful dialogue between faith and evolution requires a particular kind of relationship between knowledge ("the way we know") and reality ("the way things are"). There are those who'd argue that knowledge is all about developing categories of thought and then fitting reality into those categories (think systematic theology or various university departments). In this vein, knowledge dictates reality. Reality can never be known aside from one's interpretations of it. Objectivity remains a pipe dream. Conversely, there are others who contend that reality should dictate knowledge; that is, the "way things are" should determine "the way we know."[12] For them, objectivity is possible, if not by an individual, then certainly by enough individuals together. Get a large enough group and the biases begin to average out (just like a big sample size reduces statistical error or innumerable darting quarks in rocks collectively become subject to gravity).

"What's your point?" Dave cares but not enough to listen to me ramble on and on.

Imagine the following scenario: A sunset splashes across a snowy mountainside. Marveling at the exquisite array of color and contrast, Aunt Bernice exclaims, "How can anybody say 'there is no God'?"

"Easy," her argumentative nephew replies. "The sun sets due to the rotation of the earth. The array of colors are due to the scattering of light in the atmosphere."

Aunt Bernice exasperatingly rebuts, "Then how do you explain the beauty?"

And the nephew says, "It's an evolutionary leftover from our ancestors. Our sense of natural beauty derives from an ancient biological mechanism that drove humans to seek suitable habitats for survival."[13]

"Sure," Aunt Bernice smugly replies, "living on a snowy mountainside would have been a *great* survival strategy."

And round and round it goes.

My point is that the sunny and snowy mountainside itself does not force a specific interpretation. Reality itself does not depend upon our ability to know it. While perceptual capacity and personal bias clearly are factors when it comes to making sense of reality, they are not determinants of the reality itself. God was there before anybody believed in him. Evolution occurred before Darwin boarded *The Beagle* and sailed to the Galapagos Islands. God is not a product of faith any more than evolution is a product of science. So to say that God and evolution are at odds is an interpretative statement, not one that the realities themselves dictate since both existed *together* before interpretation was possible.

We do have to take observers' involvement into consideration whenever we talk about the human need to make sense of things. (Even if the "need to make sense of things" is *nothing but* a biological need it would still be one naturally given by God so that people could believe in him.) When it comes to knowing what's real, we cannot remove ourselves from the equation. The way we see affects how we see. But neither affect *what* we see. Reality exists however we understand it (and even when we don't). Perception may be subjective, but the thing we perceive isn't. Just because you have to explain a joke to some people doesn't mean it wasn't a joke (even if it wasn't funny). Just because people can't see infrared light or hear a dog whistle doesn't mean that infrared light doesn't exist or that dogs can't whistle (that was a joke).

Reality exists independent of me. But knowledge of reality is never independent of me.[14] We have to be honest with our own biases and proclivities. I believe God exists (even though nobody has ever seen him; 1 John 4:12). I believe that quarks exist too (nobody has seen them either). My belief in God affects my view of nature. My beliefs about nature affect my belief in God because I believe God reveals himself in nature. And because I believe God reveals himself in nature, this makes evolution a part of God's revelation. Therefore to study evolution is to further understand God. And what I understand about God helps me better understand evolution. Christian theology doesn't have to submit to accurate scientific findings, only to account for them. Authentic faith strives to believe in *what is* rather than in what we wish was. All truth is God's truth, however you look at it and whether you like it or not.

God is infinite and independent reality. Even when we know everything we can know about him, there will still be infinitely more to know. This is what makes theology so interesting. Every time we think we have God figured out, some experience or new realization comes along that unmasks our convictions as idols in need of breaking. It's what makes science so interesting too. The natural world resists our expectations that it function as we predict, forcing us to adjust our expectations in ways we'd never imagine and to extend our boundaries of comprehension.[15] In a sentence: both God and his world as science unveils it continually blow our minds.

"So then, why do science and faith remain at such odds?" Dave wondered.

A Hierarchy of Knowing

Theology and science, while complementary (at least for the believer), do not do the same thing. Science and nature are limited by space and time. Evolution addresses those processes and chains of events evident within space and time. God, on the other hand, knows no cosmological time limits, aside from whatever he imposes upon himself. And thus theology is free to explore causation and explanation that transcend temporal boundaries.

"Now what are you talking about?" Sounded to Dave as though I was back to erecting that old dividing wall.

Actually I was thinking more of a tower. Imagine knowledge as a hierarchy, a stack of intellection with disciplines devoted to component parts, such as physics, chemistry, and biology, at the bottom and disciplines devoted to the combinations of those components, such as psychology and anthropology, toward the top. Some realities require moving up the hierarchy to clarify. While fully capable of explaining the activity of atoms and light or genes and variation at their own level, physics and biology do not fully capture the complexity existent at higher-level explanations. For example, evolutionary biology cannot fully account for different tastes in music. You need psychology and musicology to do that (though there's no accounting for some tastes in music).

Go back to the food and nutrient relationship. The study of individual nutrients works fine at the chemistry level, but if you're looking for a fuller understanding of food, you have to go up to higher levels that address diet (physiology) and culture (anthropology) and Zagat's restaurant reviews (gastronomy). Again, studying the behavior of individual genes by themselves ignores the entities that emerge once genes make proteins and affect the development or diminishment of traits. Even though you can trace a trait back to its component parts, knowing about the parts still won't suffice to explain the trait. Behavior is more than a cluster of proteins.

I'm not arguing that meals are irreducibly complex,[16] just that reduction has explanatory limits. Food *is* comprised of its constituent properties that evolved over time from lesser combinations to more complex combinations through variation with natural selection (remember that pest-resistant corn). But evolution, while sufficient for explaining food's origins and development, isn't sufficient to explain all the ways food functions in your mouth or in a supermarket or at a party, each of which are essential to fully understand what food gets eaten and why.

Explanations offered at higher levels (diet and God) can be said to "supervene"[17] (which is kind of like *impose* without being rude) over lower-level explanations (nutrients and evolution) without the lower-level explanations being considered false, insignificant, or irrelevant.[18] Dietary considerations don't negate nutritional concerns (perhaps more calcium would be good for you), but whether a person picks milk or broccoli for their calcium is unanswerable at the nutrient level. Faith in God does not mean that evolution is false any more than evolution proves God does not exist. The randomness and trial and error of evolutionary progress need not imply that the universe is a crapshoot. Randomness can have a reason, which theology can explain, even if theology does not elucidate the specifics of genetic mutation.

Reality is truly multidimensional. Atoms and genes occur as do beauty and goodness. Physics and biology say plenty about atoms and genes but stumble to adequately explain beauty and goodness. But throw in psychology, ethics, and theology, and a more complete picture emerges. This supervenient hierarchy of knowing follows the ways things are in nature. Atoms combine to give rise to molecules and genes. Molecules and genes give rise to organisms, personalities, communities, cultures, and beliefs to compellingly display the "hierarchal fruitfulness" of creation itself.[19]

"Can we supervene down to the Super Burger?" Dave's peckishness had given way to full-throttled hunger.

Perspective

All I'm trying to say is that theology can embrace scientific discovery without insisting that science buy theology's presuppositions and without theology succumbing to science's own predilections. Faith allows for a perspective greater than human perception can muster, but this is never to deny the perspective that human perception *can* muster. We need not discount scientific discovery on religious grounds, even when we do take issue with scientific explanations as insufficient to paint the complete picture.

Science does not insist on a meaningless universe (even if some scientists do), only that the universe itself suggests no meaning.[20] Thus, since science does not rule out meaning, to interpret the universe as a manifestation of God's purposes is plausible. That evolution has resulted in the emergence of intelligent persons makes the claim that God made people in his own image completely rational, even if it took him thirteen billion years or so to get there.

"But why did it take God thirteen billion years to get to making people?" Dave wondered, anxious that it might take that long to get to making lunch. "That *is* an awfully long time to reach what is purportedly the pinnacle of the created order. But then again, why would God need a week? I guess knowing how humans would end up ruining everything, why hurry?"

"Who knows why God would wait so long? That is a *theological* mystery (although from God's timeless vantage point, a billion years are like a single day; Ps 90:4). But this is no *scientific* mystery. You'd need thirteen billion years or so for the universe to cool and the earth to form and things to organize enough to give way to life."

"Well, that's kind of obvious." Dave is a keen observer of the obvious. "But answer me this, why did God make people at all?"

Now *that* would be a *scientific* mystery. The scientific assumption is that were you to start over from the Big Bang, chances are that a whole different outcome would emerge. But *theologically* speaking, God's intention to make people in his own image for the purpose of relationship with them means that no matter how many times you start the universe, you'd always end up with humans, since that was what God intended.

In the end, any effort to speak adequately about the full nature of nature strains intellectual resources to the limit, whether the resources are theological or scientific. However, that science seems to do its part with less difficulty is only because science has more clear-cut boundaries than does theology. Science limits itself to the natural, measurable world while theology expands to include the immeasurable too. Everything science investigates is subject to scrutiny and testing, but when it comes to God, our posture is to be one of deference and obedience.[21] As the Lord said to Job, "Where were you when I laid the foundation of the earth? Tell me, if you have understanding" (Job 38:4). In this regard, theology is at a distinct disadvantage, scientifically speaking. Yet that we can even conceive of God is phenomenal—no less phenomenal than our ability to conceive of a universe thirteen billion years in the making. If nothing else, thinking about these things should inspire a little more awe and prevent us from speaking of God too easily.[22]

CHAPTER 5

BELIEVOLUTION

A Competent Creator

I heard a good joke recently. A scientist tells God that he's figured out how to create life from the dust of the ground, just like God did in the beginning. Consequently, the scientist says, he's shown that God is no longer a plausible hypothesis for the origin of life. Impressed, the Lord tells the scientist to do it again; he'd like to watch. So the scientist picks up a handful of dirt. But the Lord stops him right there.

"Uh-uh," God says. "Get your own dirt."

No joke: the "ground," from which Genesis declares trees sprouted, as well as people and animals (Gen 2:7, 9, 19) was *excellent* dirt. It lacked none of the resources required to pull off what biological history reveals truly happened. God packed the dirt (by which I mean all the atoms and elements of existence) with sufficient power to produce every physical structure and life form that appeared over time.[1] God endows the universe from the beginning with the potential for life—with essence, being, and "breath" (2:7; the Hebrew word for breath, wind, and spirit). God brought created reality into reality, sustaining creation as it continually unfolds to fulfill the potential woven into its fabric. Some may insist that any natural explanation of nature naturally excludes God. But that is an illogical deduction. If you're willing to affirm God as the Author of nature, God becomes the natural source of nature's ability to do all that it does. The Creator is not at odds with his creation. Rather, "the earth is the LORD's, and everything in it" (Ps 24:1 NIV).

We instinctively thank God for the *outcomes* of natural processes—mountaintops, sunsets, springtime, peaches, and newborn babies—but the processes themselves are truly marvelous too. Creation's capacity for generating beauty and life displays God's own ingenuity and generosity. We should be thanking God for the way nature works—from the intricacies of the tiniest particles to the immensities of the grandest galaxies, as well as for the precision along which all of this runs. Creation displays enormous creativity. Our constant discoveries of nature's capacities inspire, as well as defy, human imagination. What better portrayal of God is there? Stardust materializes into earth-dust, which then enlivens into organic existence. From where else (Who else?) could such creativity emerge? The Lord generously endows such resourceful potential into the universe that it succeeds in accomplishing its richness without gaps.[2] God leaves no holes. He is a competent Creator (Zech 8:12).

Ironically, it is God's competence that seems to threaten human faith most. For God to be *so* capable implies that his work is done and that no further intervention is necessary. If no further intervention is necessary, maybe the Deists[3] are right in saying God checked out after lighting the Big Bang fuse. God doesn't care about his creation now that he's got it going. But why would sufficiency without further intervention imply that God doesn't care anymore? Is shoddy work a sign of love? What kind of loving and intelligent designer would program his work to need constant repair? No artist completes a masterpiece only to despise it. Why does it make believers feel better to have the Lord pop in on biological history from time to time and supernaturally zap a new genus or two to keep things rolling? Wouldn't it be better to say that God did it right to begin with?

To acknowledge the Lord as the Maker of heaven and earth but then insist that he tweak what he's made to keep it on track, suggests that God as Maker isn't as adept as we'd presume him to be. Either that or God, the All-Powerful Creator, intentionally shortchanges his creation to give himself something to do. But that doesn't sound right either. A *natural* explanation is not a *godless* explanation because *God made nature.* The natural world is evidence of his mind-blowing skill.

God's competence does not negate intervention. God does intervene after creation, but his intervention is not to repair, but to relate. Having made his world, he intends to enjoy it, not abandon it. Maybe a better word than *intervention* would be the word *involvement.* Instead of a God who pops in to fix, how about a God who is present all the time? Lutherans use the language of "in, with and under" to describe God's presence in the bread and wine of communion. God is at the table, even though your tongue can't taste the difference. The same with God's involvement in creation. The Lord is present "in, with and under" the natural world, loving and sustaining it in all of its natural splendor.

This is the beauty of creation. God's involvement is continual and constant rather than sporadic and dramatic (as if nature itself didn't produce enough drama). The historic Christian doctrine of creation affirms that God remains present, by his Spirit, breathing life in continuous fashion, nourishing the world in all of the ways that science describes (Ps 135:6-7). Now, none of this is to suggest that the God who is involved in the natural world *never* intervenes. It's just that his intervention is not always miraculous. Rain after a long drought, a successful operation, the Red Sox winning the World Series, falling off your bike but not going over the embankment—all are wonderful (and natural) testimonies of grace.

Nor is this to suggest that miracles never happen. They do. It's just that much of what we describe as *miraculous* is more precisely *wonderful*. Miracles, you'll remember, fall into that category of supernatural providence (with the emphasis still on the natural since miracles are within the nature of God).[4] Miracles convey some deeper message than could have been communicated otherwise.[5] Miracles are a suspension of nature's laws which God alone can do since God is the Lawmaker (and never a lawbreaker). Miracles are thus unmistakable signs of God. They make no scientific sense, which is why science has nothing to say about them (at least nothing nice). Science must simply marvel at them alongside everybody else.

Of course, God makes no scientific sense either, even though his works do. Science fails to see God in his works because its methods focus solely on what can be manipulated and measured. Because God can be neither manipulated nor measured, he remains *scientifically* absent. But that's nothing new. Faith has always been required to know God (Heb 11:6). Faith is required to know the natural world as a *creation*. Science's reductionist methods, while helpful tools, cannot fully capture nature's beauty and wonder. Prose and poetry don't always succeed either, which may be why so many of the biblical writers regularly resorted to praise. As the psalmist sang, "When I look at the night sky and see the work of your fingers—the moon and the stars you have set in place—what are mortals that you should think of us, mere humans that you should care for us?" (Ps 8:3-4 NLT).

Better to praise God than to fumble with inadequate analogies. While concepts such as Engineer, Designer, or Artist have some approximate value, they never do the Creator justice. The Creator is so unique that he challenges every human comparison. Creation challenges human comprehension too—including scientific comprehension.[6] For all that science effectively describes, there is exceedingly more that remains unknown. And even the stuff that is known is never exhaustively understood. People and their knowledge-enterprises are inherently limited—science and theology included.

But again, just because we can't know everything does not mean we can't know something. God reveals himself that we might know him. God reveals himself in nature, which means he reveals himself in evolution too. We praise God for creation; why not praise God for creatively wiring the world to evolve life? Especially when it happens to work just like he wired it? The *how* and *what is* of evolutionary history portrays the *who* for whom faith provides the true identity. God is the ingenious and generous Instiller of astonishing fruitfulness into the universe.[7] God launches a universe into existence that is itself full of potential—rich, vibrant, and capable of becoming stars and planets, rocks and mountains, birds and bees, you, me, Dave, and Aunt Bernice. Such a God comes off not as distant and uninvolved but as majestic and awesome and masterful. God involves his whole self in creation: Father, Son, and Holy Spirit. The Father's will determines to create. The Son, the Word (John 1:1, 3), speaks creation into being. The Spirit too, "hovering over the waters" (Gen 1:2 NIV), is the "breath of life" (1:30) that animates the spoken material into breathing existence. The entire creation is an act of the entire Trinity.

True, the Trinity smacks of polytheism to some and celestial, mathematical nonsense to others, but for Christians it exists as the fulcrum for our entire understanding of God (even while we don't understand it—there's that mystery thing again). Christians can't *explain* the Trinity any more than scientists can explain the standard model of quantum mechanics. But this is good. The Trinity, because it defies human explanation, therefore defies human control and exploitation. Again, faith is required. Understanding follows, but understanding, when it comes to God, is always fueled by faith. Science debunks faith, because it's not derived from material evidence, and labels it prescientific, unscientific, or even antiscientific. But faith is none of these things. If anything, faith is merely *nonscientific*.[8] It knows what it knows differently than science does. Science shapes the way we think about the *works* of God, but to think of God in the first place is always a move of faith.

Creation as Relationship

For Christians, faith in God as Trinity means faith in God as personal (or as I mentioned before, *tri-personal*). God exists in eternal relationship. As personal, God could never be detached from his creation. As personal, God cares for creation. The Trinity is an eternal relationship of persons, a three-in-one community of love so bound together yet so abounding that the love happily spills over into a creation that God can't help but love too. Created by God, his creation bears the mark of relationality. Everything in nature is interconnected. The relational God creates a relational creation as an expression of himself.[9]

Science shows this relationality to be the case (as the faithful would expect). Nature, as science describes it, exists as an interconnected dynamic. From quark to quasar, from bacteria to Aunt Bernice, everything depends on everything else.[10] The fossil record details common ancestry. Anatomy, the proliferation of four limbs and two eyes across mammalian and reptilian species for instance, demonstrates relatedness. The genetic record shows that all creatures great and small share common DNA. The biochemistry of life functions basically the same way in every living thing. The elements from which all things are made materialized out of ancient starbursts. Believers would expect such commonality of origin and function if all things come from God.

In addition to commonality, there's also cooperation. Traditionally biologists have assumed a one-to-one correspondence between an individual's efforts and its evolutionary rewards, sort of evolution as "reaping what you sow" or "getting what you pay for." While this is certainly the case for moths (for instance), which go through life as evolutionary loners, it does not apply to ants, veritable evolutionary party animals (or at least evolutionary *socialists*, since I'm not sure that ants have any fun).[11] The fact is, there are many instances where an individual organism's success relies on others. Symbiosis, an increasingly recognized factor of evolution, displays the necessity of relationship between species. Everybody needs somebody if you're going to keep that gene pool flowing. Take a boxer crab and small sea anemones. The crab will wave a couple of stinging-tentacle anemones in his claws like pom-poms to scare off his enemies. The anemone benefits from the food bits that the slob of a crab drops while eating. But symbiosis is not just about mutually beneficial relationships. Parasitic and predator-prey relationships also count (though I doubt the prey consider it to be much of a relationship). Add climates and ecosystems to the mix and it's easy to imagine how relationality runs throughout the entire natural order.

Relationality shows up in the small stuff too. When it comes to our DNA, we're used to thinking that half of our genes come from our mother and the other half from our father (my mother would say the *better* half came from her). And that's basically true. But there's also a third contributor to our heritage (nothing kinky, I promise). As it turns out, some genes come from structures called *mitochondria*. These mitochondria may once have been free-living bacteria.[12] So while you can trace your genes back to your parents and their ancestry, you also have to trace mitochondrial DNA back through your mother to an interaction between your own ancestral cells and ancient bacteria (a relative that shows up on few family trees). Rather than some random mutational accident, the evolution of mammalian cells evidently occurred as some kind of symbiotic assimilation for the sake of a common mission,[13] namely to "be fruitful and multiply" (Gen 1:22). This mission also exhibits the relational nature of creation. The evidence is clear that with few exceptions (bacteria, for instance), asexual species quickly go extinct.[14] Organisms need suitable helpers—it is not good for a gene to be alone!

That relationality runs throughout the universe adds wonderful color to the biblical portrait of creation. Like the Trinity, science paints creation as a portrait of both unity and diversity.[15] Spread people onto the canvas and God's Trinitarian character emerges in even stronger relief. As God exists in face-to-face relationship with himself in community, so he crafts people in his image to enjoy the same kind of relationship with each other and ultimately with God.

What does it mean for God to "love the world"? I mean aside from Jesus coming to redeem the world (made necessary after humans screwed up the world). Presumably God loved the world *before* we made a mess of things. Some argue that to love means a cosmos free of any rigid determinism. Love does not force order but lets things be in a way that allows the objects of love to "become themselves"[16] (though I would not recommend this as a parenting philosophy). Some will protest that love as "letting be" is not really love but a Beatles song. To "let it be" smacks of divine *indifference*. Yet there's a big distinction between being indifferent and being impartial, even if both end up looking similar. Unlike human love, which struggles to love without bias, preferring one over another for all sorts of reasons, God by definition is "no respecter of persons" (Acts 10:34 KJV). He shows no partiality (Deut 10:17), loving everybody the same. In this vein, some theologians suggest that "letting be" (or "setting free" if you prefer a song by Sting) is the highest kind of love because it makes space for the other to fully emerge.[17] Viewing God's love to some extent as "setting free" would help make theological sense of evolution's apparent randomness. That evolution theoretically moves as it will for the goal of "being fruitful and multiplying" could be read as an outcome of God's creative and loving "letting be."

The Long and Winding Road

For all of God's infusing creation with its potential to become what it has become, it remains the case that the ends toward which nature has moved are not necessarily the ends toward which it *had* to move. According to the theory, light a Big Bang fuse again, and everything could turn out completely differently. Because evolution does not run in a linear fashion, purposefulness and direction can only be inferred *post hoc*. But hypothetically observed from the front end (I say "hypothetically" due to restrictions on time travel), evolution appears completely haphazard with no obvious direction or predetermined goal. And this is not just the case when talking about the uncertain movement of quarks, the unpredictable variation of genes, or the coming and going of so many traits and species. Toss in ice ages, volcanoes, meteors, and plain old inclement weather, and it's easy to see why some scientists and philosophers label ours a genuinely godless universe. But what if what looks like unpredictability is instead an inability of the human mind to perceive the logic that's there? God's ways are not our ways (Isa 55:8) and thus our failure to see a purpose in evolution does not mean that there actually is none. The apostle Paul affirms that Christ, in whom God made all things, "holds all creation together" (Col 1:17 NLT). He holds together even what looks haphazard.

Randomness can contribute to an overarching purpose. Consider a Las Vegas analogy.[18] Honest casino operators go into business based on the computational odds that a given number of random dice rolls (or card plays or roulette spins) will at the end of the day guarantee a profit. If a casino operator can use randomness (and eager gamblers) to achieve a profitable goal, how much more could God use randomness to accomplish his purposes (Prov 16:33)?[19]

Evolution allows that nature could have turned out differently than it did. But the fact that it did *not* turn out differently, that evolution actually moved from simplicity toward greater complexity and climaxed with humanity, allows purpose and intentionality (rather than purely randomness) onto the (craps) table. I'm not saying that there's no unpredictability, just that what looks like pure randomness may have a reason. Take flipping a coin. If I flip a coin to decide where to eat dinner, there's no doubt the coin flip's *outcome* has a purpose even if the coin flip itself does not.[20] A coin flip is a purely random event, which is precisely what makes it so helpful for choosing between equally desirable or undesirable options. In the Bible, random events like coin flips are used to accomplish divine purposes. People cast lots to make decisions and accept the unpredictable outcomes as God's will (1 Chr 25:8; Acts 1:26). Physically, the natural world may not display a *discernible* purpose of its own. But that does not negate the *indiscernible* purposes of God. There is no such thing as theological randomness.

However, the random aspects of the physical universe aren't totally arbitrary. Evolution's freedom occurs within limits. The indeterminate nature of quarks and genetic mutations functions according to determinate laws of nature. The eventual appearance of carbon and other heavy chemical elements depended upon the precision tuning of the universe's fundamental interactions and a specific rate of expansion (remember the anthropic principle).[21] Budge the math by even a smidgen, and you wouldn't be reading this book. Neither you nor this book would be here (but it is and you are, so keep reading). Life wouldn't exist if not for the cosmic features being precisely in place as they are, fixed in the first microseconds following the Big Bang.[22]

Surprisingly, some scientists seem to pay little attention to these strict physical constants[23] even though they underlie their own evolutionary processes.[24] It's as if these scientists take the dirt for granted. Perhaps wary of anything that smacks of intentionality, some scientists prefer to stick with the hit-and-miss nature of natural selection.[25] Ironically, however, the natural selection part of evolution is not hit-and-miss. Remember, evolution's first step, genetic variation, is visibly haphazard; but for evolution to happen, it needs something to rein in the randomness. Genetic variation by itself would only cause organic chaos and species extinction, since most genetic mutations are harmful and many are lethal. Natural selection, evolution's step 2, is needed to select which variations help and which do not based on each one's ability to enhance environmental fitness. Natural selection is not random but survival-specific. For a mutation to become a characteristic, it has to mesh with an organism's physical and social surroundings, as well as contribute to the organism's survival and reproductive capabilities.[26]

The determining nature of natural selection on genetic variation also works internally. Genetic variation depends on the genes that are already present, a result of prior natural selection's conservation of successful variations. When variation occurs, through either reproduction or mutation, natural selection conserves the new and otherwise impossible genetic *combinations* and passes them down through the generations.[27] This conservation over the course of biological history places boundaries on the chance processes. You can't mutate what you don't have. Spin a roulette wheel and the odds are fresh every spin because roulette wheels have no memory. What happened in the past has no effect on the future. But natural selection is not roulette. Prior spins count toward the final jackpot. Chance traits that get selected are assimilated into an organism's makeup and thereby affect future development.

Granted, saying that natural selection *determines* evolution is not the same as saying that the selection process itself was predetermined. This is why Darwin called it *natural* selection. It happens naturally without anybody pulling the levers. Darwin rightly worried that his theory would upset the faithful. He figured that evolution meant God was not there.

But again, *natural* selection need not imply *godless* selection. Gravity could be described as godless too. You could say that gravity's lack of grace (airplanes crash and people fall to their deaths) demonstrates that God does not exist. But gravity has never caused any believer to lose sleep (unless of course you or yours were one of those who tragically fell to their deaths). Evolution by natural selection is no more godless than gravity. In fact, you could also say that gravity demonstrates God's constancy and impartiality, like the sun, which shines on the righteous and unrighteous alike (Matt 5:45).[28] If gravity can be interpreted as evidence for God's constancy and fidelity, why can't evolution be a sign of God's ingenuity and generosity?

Freedom and Progression

Though you can't predict an evolutionary trend from nature's front end, you can look back through history and see a progression.[29] And the observed progress has bent toward increasing overall complexity, particularly with regard to human consciousness. Scientists puzzle over the evolution of human consciousness (the experiencing of ourselves as experiencing selves) due to its mystifying nature. Its emergence is an extraordinary, and so far inexplicable, evolutionary outcome. One reason for the puzzlement of consciousness is that even the four billion plus years of earth-time doesn't seem to be enough time for nondirectional evolution to fully account for the human mind.[30] If evolution is the process at work, it is remarkable that such a process would lead to human self-consciousness.[31] So remarkable, in fact, that to think consciousness could evolve without evolution having been a tool of God stretches biology to the brink.[32]

Does a *post hoc* view of progress toward greater complexity and the emergence of human consciousness mean that evolution is *directional* even if there is no discernibly detailed roadmap? Science could never say that. However, theologically, the fact that human evolution *has* traveled the course that it has can be readily explained by God's involvement. Acting "in, with and under" evolutionary processes, God himself invisibly directs the course of biological history in all of its beauty and intricate wonder.[33] Inasmuch as the universe exhibits an intrinsic relatedness, we might go on to say that evolution's progression represents a striving toward ever deeper relationship—an actualization of the relational potential God infused into creation's existence. Whether this is happening, science cannot say. But faith can shout it from the rooftops.[34]

Still, how does theology justify the evident randomness that nevertheless plays a part? Leaving aside for a moment the possibility that randomness is an aberration of human perception, if God purposefully made the heavens and the earth to move accidentally, what purpose does the randomness serve? Even if the casino analogy applies and God used chance toward a predetermined or highly probable end, why not just get on with it instead of leaving room for deviation along the way?

Theologians (and the Beatles) commonly appeal to love. As a loving God, he could not have forced creation into what he wanted it to be and called it love. A loving and relational God would want to instil creation with a level of freedom and autonomy in order for it to become sufficiently "other" than himself. You can't have a relationship of love with yourself. (True, as tri-personal, God is able to be in relationship with himself. But to elevate creation to a similar level would be to declare creation divine, something Christian theology has consistently opposed.) But is "letting be" the only way to love? Surely guiding a free creation toward purposeful ends is not an unloving act (otherwise all parents are tyrants). Yet if God guides the process, why allow things to take so long? Some think that maybe the freedom God allows in the system is for the sake of creaturely exploration.[35] Maybe it doesn't matter to God whether sparrows look exactly the way they do. Maybe it would have been OK had they evolved differently, with bigger wings or longer beaks. What matters is that God knows and loves them, however they turned out (Luke 12:6). Sparrows enjoyed the freedom to evolve as they did.

OK, so I know that sounds a little goofy (what sparrow wouldn't prefer to be an eagle?), but the idea is not unlike the way we personally experience our own human freedom under God. While at times we may speak of God's will in terms of a detailed plan, our experience is more often that of a range of possibilities. We decide to take a job as an engineer, a chemist, or a dog walker based on personal assessment, preference, and variables such as salary levels and what might please Mom and Dad. Choosing between a psychology major or a business major, marrying this person or that—all of these are choices we make of our own free will (as far as we can tell). Even the decision to believe in God is a choice freely made (Rom 10:10-13). However, just because every human choice, process and outcome are not divinely predetermined (as far as we can tell), does not mean such choices, processes, and outcomes are not a part of God's will.

Rather than viewing the will of God as akin to a tightrope (one false move and you're doomed), what if instead God's will resembles a one-way, six-lane highway? The direction is determined, but the manner of getting there (what you drive, which lane you travel, and how fast you go) is a function of creaturely freedom. There are a lot of ways you can do "love your neighbor." Or to borrow another analogy, what if God is like a grand master chess player playing with an eight-year-old novice?[36] The game has its rules and regularities (created by God), such that whatever move the eight-year-old makes, the grand master already knows its outcome. There's no doubt who will win in the end. Likewise, with human freedom and evolutionary processes (the eight-year-old novices in this analogy), God knows what will happen in any scenario with any moves that are made. He can make any of them work for his victory. Whether driving metaphorical cars or playing analogous chess, creatures and creation freely exercise the grace and ability God gives to do what God wants done. As creatures we participate in the Creator's purposes. This too reflects God's communal personality. As a trinitarian God, Father, Son, and Holy Spirit all take part in creating and sustaining the universe. Likewise the creation itself as a manifestation of God's nature, participates in what God is doing. The creation "creates" as it were, empowered by God and interacting with all the other parts for the sake of God's purposes.

Evolution's exploratory and emergent processes suggest a God for whom and toward whom creation is *called*. Nature and its processes freely respond to the lure of God's love. Christians will describe this in terms of obedience—that way of life that joyfully conforms to the purposes for which it was intended. From a scientific vantage point, nature appears to go where it will. But from theology's vantage point, nature freely goes where God wills.

A God who presides in such fashion over unfolding reality is not a god for Deists. He is ingeniously and generously (if mysteriously) involved filling existence with the resources and promise to become what God knew it could become.[37] We can still ask *why* it took so long and *why* it happened the way it did, but that it took as long and happened as it did is not to deny God's hand in it. Of course, you could also spin it around and suggest that the thirteen billion years it *did* take to make the world as we know it is just another example of God's generosity.[38] That he would allow for such a lavish expenditure of time, energy, resources, and space to bring about the origin of earth and the eventual emergence of people emphasizes anew how much God so loved the world. Not only did he suffer and die to redeem it, but he spent whatever it took to make it in the first place.

If it sounds like I'm working too hard to make God compatible with evolution, I'm not. Faith does not have to account for or justify every event in natural and human history. Nor does faith have to explain every scientific finding that seems to contradict what theology teaches. Faith does not demand that God act like we think he should act, whether it's to abide by our schedules, follow our rules, or perform according to our expectations.[39] God does as he pleases because it pleases him to do it his way (Ps 115:3). There's no reason to think that everything that has occurred didn't occur according to God's plan. It just may be that God's plan doesn't look like we thought it would.

Of course, the place where we get our ideas about God's plan is the Bible. Scripture isn't typically interpreted to grant quite as much leeway to creation as evolution appears to require. The Bible can be read to portray God as direct and meticulous as to the specifics of his creating the heavens and the earth. But again, the nonnegotiable aspect of the creation narrative is to affirm the *who* and the *why* more than the *how*. Clearly the biblical authors would have had no working concepts of gravity, quantum indeterminacy, genetic variability, or natural selection— even though these things existed. To expect the Bible to speak to the particulars of evolution as a natural process of God seems unwarranted (just as we wouldn't expect the Bible to speak of general relativity or electron configuration).[40] However, Scripture rightly gives us the portrayal of the universe as a *creation*. To properly understand the universe as creation, Scripture must accompany scientific discovery. And because the universe is a creation, we should expect Scripture, correctly interpreted, to agree with scientific discovery (given that the science is correctly interpreted too).[41] Both come from God and tell us what we need to know about God.

Reading Nature and the Bible Together

How about another joke?

A zookeeper is walking his morning rounds when he notices an orangutan reading two books, the Bible and Darwin's *The Origin of Species.* Surprised, the zookeeper asks, "Why are you reading both those books?"

The orangutan replies, "I wanted to know if I was my brother's keeper or my keeper's brother."

So, what about the disagreements between science and the Bible? If all truth is God's truth, shouldn't Scripture and science, correctly interpreted, basically agree? What happens when they don't? Generally speaking, conflict between confirmed scientific data and the biblical interpretation of scientific data may indicate a need to rethink one's interpretation.[42] This is not a bad thing. Belief in an infallible Bible does not render its readers infallible. Given that in the Bible God chose to show himself in a particular time, place, and culture (even though the implications apply across all time, places, and cultures), we should not expect Scripture to comment specifically on the topics of modern science any more than we should expect it to comment specifically on things like modern architecture or how to manage an investment portfolio (though that would have been helpful). This is not to say we cannot extrapolate principles and values from Scripture and convert them into modern practice; we do this all the time (even with investment portfolios, Jesus' admonition against storing treasures on earth notwithstanding). But any interpretive move from ancient to modern culture happens provisionally. Human perspective, limitation, and error must always be factored in.

The same is true with science. If we go back to that knowledge tower, physics and biology operate on the ground levels, deciphering the basic materials of existence as they are expressed in nature. Fully capable at their own level to explain physical and biological activity, they cannot completely depict the complexity that emerges at higher levels of explanation. Basic science has its limits. Disciplines such as psychology, anthropology, sociology, and theology are needed to round out the whole picture. Because all truth is God's truth, we can appreciate science's contribution to theological accuracy as we can trust theology's contribution to the meanings behind scientific discovery.

Theology's beef is not with the things that science discovers but with the way some scientists interpret what science discovers. Just as an atheist and a theist will differ on the meaning of Genesis, so an atheist and a theist will argue about the implications of genetic variation for the purposes of God. But that genes actually mutate should not be debated. We know that genetic variation occurs. Contention is unnecessary insofar as confirmed scientific findings are what they are. The same with a well-attested biblical text (by which I mean the actual document itself, the words written on the parchment). The text says what it says even if there is divergence over what the text means.[43] Interpretations of scientific data and biblical texts and their mutual effect on each other may always be fodder for deliberation, but in any discussion involving faith and science, both the data and the text can be treated with equal seriousness.

Interestingly, it was Genesis 1 that initially laid the intellectual groundwork for science.[44] Genesis' assertion of God as Creator implied that order and unity underlay nature. This assumption of nature's consistency (grounded in the integrity of God), led early scientists to design experimental processes that would assess nature's constancy and predict its outcomes. That early scientists actually found the sorts of trustworthy things that they expected to find only affirmed their faith in the constancy and trustworthiness of God.

Nature functions as God's "word" in similar ways that Scripture does: both convey divine character. However, this does not mean that both nature and science get read the same way. The book of Genesis isn't set up to provide technical accounts of the chemical origins of the universe, but it does succeed as a framework for the rest of biblical revelation. Reiterations of the Genesis imagery show up throughout Scripture—be it in the tabernacle and the temple, Ezekiel's visions, John's gospel-introduction, or Revelation's conclusion. These underscore God's authority over all time and all things as well as his intention to reconcile all things in Christ. That these reiterations are at times understood as literary rather than literal depictions in no way diminishes their impact. To be literary is not to lie. Ezekiel provides exacting details of a temple that was never built (nor could it have been). The takeaways from each reiteration of the creation account in Scripture serve as central reaffirmations of faith—namely God as Creator, humanity as the epitome of creation, and God as Redeemer of creation by becoming human in Christ. These affirmations then provide the interpretive lens for scientific discovery.

Genesis 1

The imagery and language of Scripture, and Genesis in particular, are nonscientific; they offer a different kind of description of the universe in accordance with vocabulary and concerns pertinent to ancient Near Eastern culture (which obviously could not have included modern science).[45] Nevertheless, as the enduring revelation of God, the imagery and language of Genesis also inform, in fuller fashion, the specifics of God's handiwork that science has uncovered. That the universe emerged thirteen billion years ago does not negate the language of six days; it simply shows us that the meaning of six days (and the all-important seventh day) is to be read differently than as a sequence of twenty-four-hour periods.

Creation Narrative

Paging through Genesis 1, you notice that creative activity is narrated topically instead of sequentially.[46] Light shows up on day 1 and vegetation on day 3, but the sun doesn't appear until day 4. In this way the creation accounts work like the gospels do, focusing more on thematic unity than on a strict chronological sequence.[47] A poetic parallelism is noticeable if days 1 to 3 are grouped in one column and then days 4 to 6 set in a column alongside. You'll read light appearing on day 1 with the sun, moon, and stars on day 4; the sea and sky on day 2 and the sea- and sky-dwellers on day 5; the land and vegetation on day 3 and the dwellers of land on day 6.[48] Day 7 is the culmination of both columns of creative work (see table below). The absence of the "evening and morning" formula suggests that the seventh day is an eternal day which has no end,[49] an idea which Scripture affirms elsewhere (Heb 4:3-11).

Day 1 Light	Day 4 Sun, moon, and stars
Day 2 Sea and sky	Day 5 Sea and sky-dwellers
Day 3 Land and vegetation	Day 6 Land-dwellers
Day 7 Rest	

Poetic Parallelism of the Creation Narrative

As for the "evening and morning" formula itself chances are that it reflects the Jewish notion of daily reckoning (a day runs from sunset to sunset). The Hebrew word for day (*yom*) means twenty-four hours in some places, but not every place. Within Genesis itself, a day can mean just twelve hours (29:7) or an indefinite period of time (35:3).[50] But again, the point here is not the chronology of creation but its authorship and purpose (as well as its dissimilarity from the pagan creation accounts that were vying for Israel's affection). The question naturally arises as to how one makes the distinction between when the Bible is being literal and when it is being literary. Remember that context is crucial. For Genesis, it can be argued that because chapters 1 and 3 don't begin with the phrase "this is the account," these earliest chapters are to be read differently than what follows (*account* meaning "read this as literal history").[51] Whether this is the case or not, the point is that Genesis itself does not demand that modern cosmological and evolutionary evidence be rejected.

Adam and Eve

My uncle told me this joke: Adam is lonely and moping around the garden, so God says to him, "I can make a companion for you. She will harvest

the garden and cook you delicious meals. She will tidy up the house and d
the dishes. When you disagree, she will always admit she's wrong first, and
she'll never have a headache." Bowled over, Adam says, "What will *tha*
cost me?" The Lord replies, "An arm and a leg." Thinking about it
Adam then counters, "What can I get for a rib?"

So what about God creating Adam out of the dirt and Eve from hi
rib? Literal or literary? Was there an actual garden with two trees? Hov
about a talking snake? Can we read Adam's origin as a poetic reference
to God's involvement in the evolution of humanity? And what abou
Eve's appearance? The description of Adam sleeping and God perform
ing a rib-ectomy to make a woman could be exactly what happened. Bu
what if instead Eve was Adam's evolved companion, chosen by God to be
Adam's wife (the first arranged marriage, if you will)? We'd still have the
biblical emphasis on the importance of marriage as a one-flesh unity.[5]
Jesus treats Genesis 2:24 in this fashion when he teaches on marriage and
divorce (Matt 19:5), and Paul relies on the passage to describe our rela
tionship to Christ as his church (Eph 5:25).[53] As for the tree of life, i
could be a real tree, or it could be a literary tree, but either way, it woul
represent communion with God in the garden as it represents heavenly
communion with God in Revelation 22 (the garden being a mirror o
heaven).[54] What about the tree of knowledge? Literal or literary, eithe
way it could be read as representative of human deviation and defiance.[5]
Faithful Christians diverge on all of this, and science clearly has no *scien
tific* opinion since a specially created first couple, an Edenic garden par
adise, and a talking serpent would be supernatural occurrences.

In trying to bring faith and evolution together (or at least have then
play nice), we could take the easy out and label Adam and Eve or the gar
den as *obviously* figurative. That's too easy, I think, and doesn't take
Scripture as seriously as it deserves. Because the Genesis 2 account o
humanity's appearance is called an *account* (2:4), it perhaps should be read
as more report than poetry; literal rather than literary. Jesus, Paul, and
others throughout Scripture all treat Adam and Eve as historical figures
As historical figures, there are basically two options for their existenc
within an evolutionary rubric.

The first is that God created them supernaturally, midstream in evo
lution's flow. To create in such a way would require that God also wire in

place a DNA history, since human origins genetically trace back to earlier, common ancestors. Conceptually, this presents the same problems as creating the universe with apparent age. Apparent age is how some square a literal Genesis with scientific evidence. Stars that *appear* to be billions of years old (according to cosmological measurements) are in reality only a few thousand years old (according to literal biblical reckoning). God created the stars with age. The problem is that creating with age makes God seem to be tricking us into thinking things are older than they are with no clear reason for doing so. Nevertheless, given that Adam and Eve are both introduced in Genesis, presumably as adults rather than children (even if they acted like children), it could be that in their case, God's creating with age (and a history) would apply. While we might not necessarily understand *why* God would do that, he *could* do that (being God and all).

Another option might be to have Adam and Eve exist as first among *Homo sapiens*, specially *chosen* by God as representatives for a relationship with him. We often speak theologically of Adam as serving as humanity's representative in matters of original sin (his sin affects us all; Rom 5:12); so the idea of Adam as representative already exists in Christian theology. Science asserts that evolved brain capacity and function are part of what set *Homo sapiens* apart from previous hominids. It is this same capacity and function that make relationship possible and, particularly in the creation account, covenantal relationships between humans and God and between humans and each other (i.e., marriage).[56] An advantage of this interpretation is that God's natural processes marvelously work without the need for any ancestral or genetic fabrication. Also, you'd finally be able to explain where it is that Cain found his wife (answer: from the other humans walking the earth east of Eden; Gen 4:16-17). Though how Adam managed to live 930 years remains a puzzler (Gen 5:5-6).

People Are Different

However, this view would require a reinterpretation in regard to words like *formed* and phrases like "breathed into his nostrils the breath of life" (Gen 2:7 KJV).[57] Can we use *formed* and *breathed* to mean "created through the long and continuous history of biological evolution" (as were the other living creatures in Genesis 1)? If so, then perhaps "the Lord God formed the man" could be read emphasizing the novelty and uniqueness which humans inhabit.[58] Similarly, the "breath of life" would not signify simply oxygenated animation (surely Genesis isn't merely speaking in that sense), but that *breath* which set humans apart as inspired by God (the Hebrew word for *breath* here is different than the word used for oxygen intake by living creatures as a whole).

Whether specially created or specially selected, humans constitute an interruption in the evolutionary process. Before people showed up, evolution's potential pathways were invisible. But once humans appear, human volition entered with it. The human capacity to choose replaced randomness with intentionality. As people, we have developed enough mastery over our environment (Gen 1:28) that natural selection, in the strict Darwinian sense, no longer applies to us. We now control our own evolution, capable not only of self-awareness but of self-determination too. Qualities that make relationship with God and others possible (reflecting the personhood-in-community of the Trinity) also made the *breaking* of relationship possible. This is a sad reality expressed throughout human history. The brokenness of human relationship affects not only our relationship with God and our relationships with each other but our relationship with the rest of creation. (Even if humans were specially created, we were still made out of the dust of the ground, the same ground from which all other living things emerged.)

We are biological organisms and share similarities with other life forms, albeit with qualitative differences.[59] Theology and science actually agree about this. Science cites language and consciousness as humanity's distinguishing characteristics. We can communicate and reason in ways that other animals do not. Theology also recognizes language and consciousness as uniquely human. They are part of what characterize people as bearers of God's image. As to language, the ability to speak resides at the center of God's own identity. God spoke creation into being with the mere mention of his word, the Word that became flesh in the person of Christ. Likewise, humans communicate through words; we speak reality into being. We can't manufacture material reality through our speech, but it is the case that words do have physical outcomes. Words hurt and they heal.

As to human consciousness, this corresponds to the spirit of God Present at the foundation of the world, the spirit hovered over the form-less waters to bring meaning and shape to the universe. Similarly, the human spirit shapes and brings meaning to its perception of the universe Consciousness enables relationship and creates community. It is the means whereby people live out their trinitarian heritage. Consciousness enables us to see ourselves as images of God. But more importantly, we are able to see others as bearing God's image too. The Bible teaches that to love God means loving our neighbor (1 John 4:20-21). As creatures who image our Creator, we are made to love one another and God as God loves us and himself (within the Trinity). This capacity to love and be loved by God, as well as loving and being loved by others in commu-nity, is often what is meant by *spirituality* or *soul*[60]

Body and Soul

The concept of *soul* has been understood religiously as that aspect of human identity that transcends earthly life. The idea is that the immate-rial soul departs from the material body at death to live an eternally con-scious and personal existence. The soul lives on (somewhere) as the material body decomposes. With the "resurrection of the body" at the second coming of Christ, transformed or re-created material bodies get reunited with the immaterial soul to craft a reunited person.[61] (Nobody s sure about what's going on in the meantime. Get it? *No body*.) By con-trast, every advance in biology, psychology, physiology, and medicine has determined an almost inextricable connection between mental activity (including all aspects of personality) and the physical organization of the human brain. If by immaterial soul we mean the essence of human iden-ity and personality (as given by God), then soul is also somehow con-nected to a functioning brain and the rest of the nervous system. This is not to say that the soul is *nothing but* brain function, but any concept of the soul being independent of the body has become scientifically suspect Scientists expect that capacities once attributed to a nonmaterial soul will turn out to be products of complex neural organization.[62]

Of course, just because the soul has become *scientifically* suspect does not prove souls are only material. Nevertheless, brain science represents a dramatic new frontier for understanding human thought and experience. The expectation is that someday thought and experience (including personal faith) will be visible as neural patterns on an MRI. Conceivably, thoughts and experiences might one day be electronically replicated or induced, perhaps even be tangible enough to hold in your hand. Already we know that genes, drugs, disease, and head trauma can dramatically influence human personality. There are genetic and biochemical, as well as environmental, factors in mental illness. Is the soul immune to such influences?[63]

What if science discovered the soul to be *purely* material, a product of evolutionary development akin to consciousness itself? Would this present an insurmountable hurdle to theology? No. Materialistic explanations of the mind and the soul present no theological problem because the material is the "dust of the ground." A material soul would still be one that was made in God's image and thus subject to his redemption at the end of time. Besides, whenever Scripture speaks of body and soul, it does so for the most part as a unified entity, that is, as an *embodied soul*. Genesis 2:7 (KJV) uses the language "living soul" (*nephesh*), but this same phrase is also used of the animals (1:20, 24, 30). It is not, then, the "soul" that sets us apart from animals, even as it links us to them. What separates us from the animals is being made in God's image as his children (Gen 5:1-3).[64]

At a minimum, soul refers to *breathing*, being alive. But in other places, the Old Testament also uses the word to designate craving or hunger, particularly for God and his righteousness (Ps 107:9; cf. Matt 5:6). So with regard to human beings, soul points toward our spirit-induced capacity (and need) for relationship with God and others. However, our relational lives are never immaterial but always full-bodied: heart, soul, mind, and strength (Deut 6:5; Mark 12:30). Jesus does make a contrast between body and soul when he speaks of people who "kill the body but cannot kill the soul" (Matt 10:28 NIV). His distinction, however, is between humans and God and not body and soul. Humans can kill the body but only God can "kill the soul." That is, only God can kill the relationship forever between himself and those who reject him. This he does by "destroy[ing] *both* soul and body in hell" (10:28 NIV; italics mine).[65] Likewise, the apostle Paul's distinction between *flesh* and *spirit* does not pit a material body (considered evil) against a disembodied and eternal soul (conceived as good). Instead, it can be read as Paul's way of distinguishing human sinfulness (flesh) from human faith and obedience (spirit; Rom 8:5).

My point in pushing all of this is not to diminish the concept of soul but simply to show that evolution and faith need not diverge at this juncture. One look at the resurrected Jesus and you see not an immaterial being but a living person. The gospels insist that the living, postmortem presence of Jesus was not the presence of a ghost but that of touchable "flesh and bones" (Luke 24:39) risen from the dead. Paul describes this same body as a "spiritual body" (1 Cor 15:44), the kind of body we ourselves will inherit at death as Christians (15:20—Christ as "the first fruits of those who have died" implies that his resurrection serves as a paradigm for and precursor of our own). As the apex and ambition of humanity, whom Scripture describes as the "second Adam," Jesus exists as the perfect picture of humanity's redemption. And thus scientific advances that reduce mind or soul down to physical brain function do not undermine what theology teaches regarding body and soul. God made us as whole body-soul persons and will redeem us as whole body-soul persons. Our physical bodies are not mere containers of our *real* selves but are themselves bound for transformation at the end of time (which is how you'll get recognized as you).

If God created the heavens and the earth and made people in his own image, as the Bible teaches, and if science is essentially right in its description of earth's formation and life's evolution then God is the God of evolution. Without God there would be no evolution. To believe in God is not to reject science any more than it is to believe that what science teaches is to reject God. Because all truth is God's truth, we expect science and theology to speak to and with one another in ways that provide comprehensive portraits of the handiwork and character of God. The tendency is to fear scientific advancement because of the presumption that each scientific advance squeezes God further out of the picture. But if God is God of all things, then each scientific advancement about nature only further illumines the nature of God.

Which should be a good thing. Right? Unless the next joke's on me.

CHAPTER 6

GOD IS GREAT, GOD IS GOOD—
BUT MAYBE I'VE
MISUNDERSTOOD?

When I consider the works of your hand, which you display in all you have created, I am at once awed and bewildered. I believe, yet sometimes I need help to believe. I wonder at your creativity, and at the same time I wonder why your creativity looks so different than I would expect. I wonder why the earth evolved instead of simply appearing, and why life has taken such a long road to get to where it is. I would have expected you to act more immediately and efficiently. Yet I know that my expectations are extensions of my own desires. And though you may be the author of my desire, I am the one who distorts it and imposes those distortions on you. I know that I must humble my understanding to your unveiling. Yet to observe your world and your ways creates a collision within my mind, a dissonance that I desperately long to resolve.

You're infinite, and I'm finite, confined within time and by my sin and thereby limited in perception and understanding. Your eternity dwarfs my capacity to comprehend it. Your holiness outshines my feeble faith. Any claim to know you sounds presumptuous. And yet as a God of love you unveil yourself so that I can know you. Revelation is part of your character. You show us yourself in order to draw us to yourself. Your work and your word extend love and beckon our response of love. Relationship is your essence and you invite us to partake of it. You are love and your love is magnificently splashed across the universe and intricately wired into our souls.

But where does my faith in this relationship come from? You wire us for relationship, but how did it happen? How is it that we humans believe? Science suggests that faith is either an adaptive mechanism or an evolutionary accident. Either it surfaced as a means of assuring survival or as a mistaken by-product of something else.[1] If science is right, I can't help but wonder if my mind is making stuff up. My faith gives me hope; is it false hope? Or is it just true fear?

Whether faith is a product (or a by-product) of evolution says nothing about the object of faith. Being wired to believe is different from being wired to believe in you, the trinitarian God. Perhaps you set us up to believe but then grant us the freedom to decide in whom to believe. You give me the capacity of relationship without imposing relationship so that my relationship with you can be genuine. Even if my faith is construed as an evolved mental ability, it is still a faith that is aimed at you. You give me faith to know and love you.

And yet underneath, uncertainty looms. Do I know you? I marvel at the beauty of your creation, but beauty comes at great cost. The stars that were exploded into place are destined to flame out in a series of massive fatalities. Our sun burns toward oblivion. The sparrows and lilies of the field, which delight us with song and splendor, do so as a consequence of epochs of struggle for survival, a struggle that persists even now. We hear music and see splendor, but those are but mechanisms for enduring a competition that pits life against life. Life itself is your gift and yet each life hardly registers as a whisper in the vastness of time. And time itself registers as barely a whisper in the vastness of eternity. I and every other living thing are but insignificant moments in an unsearchable string of moments that are swallowed up within an infinity where no moments exist.

By your power you made the heavens and the earth. You created reality, breaking open existence with divine and furious heat. The dust of the starry heavens became the dust of the earth, the dust from which you made every living thing. Yet the dust from which creation is composed, with all its glorious creatures and planets and stars, this dust amounts to a mere fraction of your creation.[2] The immeasurable remainder is darkness—dark matter—imperceptible and unquantifiable. It's as if the visible universe, and certainly our place in it, exists as a bit of cosmic pollution, an ultimately inconsequential speck. An afterthought. Were you to remove all that we can see, the universe would hardly be different. It's as if the heavens and earth are totally trivial.[3] Indeed, who *are* we that you are mindful of us, mere mortals that you should care for us (Ps 8:4)?

Yet you've made us a little lower than yourself and crowned us with glory and honor (8:5), the same glory with which you have filled the earth, but I realize that your glory casts long shadows. A holy pathos permeates the earth.[4] Our planet appears to be so insignificant and alone in the vast expanse of space and its inhabitants mimic that irrelevancy as the weak and powerless seem carelessly cast aside. In the evolution of life, you tolerate what looks like enormous amounts of cruelty and waste. Species emerge only to go extinct. Predators devour their prey. Care gives way to brutality. Is this the shape of your love, that it would expend the least of creatures in a long and tortuous evolutionary epic? If death and struggle are woven into your world, are they part of your purpose for the world? Why create life only to watch it die?

I know that evolutionary life can't occur without death. One generation must give way to the next—the circle of life and all that. But I fight to understand this in terms of my faith. Should all of this death be viewed as your unfathomable sacrifice? Your generous willingness to put all things literally under our feet (8:6)? Were you so intent on making creatures in your image and granting them a world to inhabit that you'd spend thirteen billion years of cosmic and planetary life to make it happen? All for the slight blip of relationship you enjoyed with humanity before we fell from your favor? Who are we that you would go to such lengths, not even sparing your own Son, but giving him up, and with him, giving us all things (Rom 8:32)? This *is* too great. I can't understand it. We don't deserve it.

As bearers of your image, you grant us dominion over the works of your hands (Ps 8:6). All creatures, great and small, do your bidding. You bid them die, it seems, to fuel a richness of resource in which we humans partake and depend. Billions of years of biological deterioration lavish upon us fossil fuel, but our domination of it has become a mockery of your generosity. Without organic death we wouldn't have coal and oil, but then we wouldn't have global warming and global war either. Is this your will too? Has the sacrifice of your creation been rendered meaningless by our sin? Our ingratitude and our sense of entitlement defraud your gifts. Our sin and selfishness ruin your world.

Perhaps death is the result of our own sin. The wages of sin is death (Rom 6:23) but what about death for which there was no sin? What about death due to disease or genetic deformity? I know your purposes are woven into the fabric of all things—from the enormous complexity of the cosmos that expands beyond us to the intricate complexity within us. Yet having your will woven in the quantum and genetic fabric of human existence implicates you as responsible for the disease and suffering that those genes bring about.[5] How can that be? Birth defects and prenatal congenital syndromes—could the designs of your creation be attained no other way (Exod 4:11-12)?

What about earthquakes, hurricanes, and meteoric catastrophes? Should these be construed as evil? as evidence of a groaning creation (Rom 8:22)? a fallen world due to human transgression? What about the world before it was fallen? Disaster and dying occurred throughout prehuman history; don't they trace back to your hand? You are God. You cause or allow all things. Is this your design? Time's engulfing massiveness, life's cruel thirst for survival—perhaps these indiscriminate exhibitions of cosmic power reflect a creation left too freely to its own devices. Maybe this unavoidable darkness is the long shadow cast by the light of your glory.

Must goodness depend on this shadow for its goodness?[6] Your ways, as revealed in nature, appear unbearably harsh and terrifying. Your ways in Scripture do too. I know that you terrify the sinner to retaliate against sin and to display your ferocious justice (Jer 4:6; 2 Tim 3:1). You warn the abuser and put the oppressor on notice. Death is your righteous response to human evil and defiance (Rom 5:12). But death and destruction still occur prior to humanity's appearance. Prehumans (those who existed prior to *Homo sapiens*), while devoid of your communicative spirit, have nevertheless left traces of primitive religion and culture. They suffered too. To what should we ascribe their suffering if sin (and evil) are presumably the consequences of Adam and his offspring's rebellion? What of that suffering that happens before *Homo sapiens* appear?

Perhaps we should attribute this evil to disobedient spirits, angels whose own rebellion led to their fall (2 Pet 2:4). But Satan isn't a serious rival. His powers can't compete with yours. While you permit his perversions to test human faith (Job 2:3), Satan is powerless to impede your purposes (Luke 4:13). Still, we're left with evil's presence, a senselessness that enters creation with your permission, presumably prior to our partaking in it (if I can call that snake in the garden "evil"). This puts a heavy burden on my faith: how can a God who is beneficent and omnipotent ever allow evil? If God is beneficent, he must not be omnipotent, because evil exists. If God is omnipotent, then he must not be beneficent, because evil exists. You know the argument.

But how can I attribute evil to your will (Job 34:10). You do no wrong. Can this possibly mean that the wrong I see, the suffering and the squandering of life, is *good* instead? Or is your hand detached from your handiwork? Moral evil I understand, or I should say I can attribute it to cause. Your beauty we mar, your love we defy, your will we ignore. We spew our unrighteousness all over your landscape. You made us for virtue, but we choose to follow our own downward path instead (Eccl 7:29). You gave us freedom, but we abuse that freedom. We are without excuse (Rom 1:20). Through Christ you have made the way of the cross to be the way of life; darkness and hardship are often the places where faith finds solid ground. But you never *cause* darkness and hardship? My God would never cause death and trouble. My God would never allow evil to torment. Would you?

I read my Bible and find that you do all these things. "There is no Holy One like the LORD, no one besides you; there is no Rock like our God. . . . The LORD brings death and makes alive; he brings down to the grave and raises up. The LORD sends poverty and wealth; he humbles and he exalts" (1 Sam 2:2 NRSV, 6-7 NIV). Does this mean you pick some to kill and some to make alive, some to impoverish and some to make rich, some to humble and others to exalt? To read it this way makes you seem capricious, even malicious.

But your creation *is* good, so your purposes—no matter how much I struggle to understand them—*must* be right and good too. It's you who hung the stars in their places (Ps 8:3), and it's by your will that they hang where they are. It's you who fixed the laws of nature, the physics that steers the universe. Without them precisely as they are, there'd be no life because there'd be no earth, no sun, no stars, and nothing but a big bang echoing into nothingness. And here I come up against another dilemma. The laws by which the universe exploded into being and continues its course are the same laws that destine the universe for either a deep fry or a deep freeze. You created the universe with an abrupt and final end in mind, long before sin ever appeared. Has your plan always been to doom your creative work to disastrous finality?

The precision tuning of nature and the exactitude of your physical laws not only assure creation's decimation, but likewise they assure creaturely suffering. For us to exist, the perfection of nature had to inflict its damage.[7] Is this your love, or are you really indifferent? Do you begin things only to step back and allow them to run their own catastrophic course? You infused potentiality into creation, yet it runs up against so many dead ends over the course of its evolutionary development. The variations and mutations that compose organic life most often conspire to destroy it. Their emergence disorders your order so that harm and lethality prove more common than adaptation does. This seems so meaningless. Some might argue that "letting be" is a supreme character of your love. Yet such letting be feels more like "letting go." The only other alternative is for creation to be an accidental afterthought, a senseless by-product, devoid of any hope besides what we fabricate for ourselves.

But then I take a closer look at your handiwork and recognize that *accidental* isn't really a word that applies. For instance, plenty of people argue that the chance origination of any particular protein molecule is inconceivably improbable. If you take twenty different amino acids and attempt to randomly construct a protein chain of a hundred, even shuffling one billion times per second would require many times the history of the universe to sort though all the possible combinations.[8] And yet this is the foundation of life. Doesn't this improbability enlist the necessity of your hand?

I'm thrown back to your hand as the source of organic mishap—genetic deformity, disease, and dysfunction. Unless DNA and RNA or mindless cells and bacteria are purposeful agents, who else are we supposed to blame? Is this what's meant by original sin? Or should we view this as an act of divine sovereignty and accept it with silence? Although you're the Holy One who kills and makes alive, who wounds and heals (1 Sam 2:6), you aren't deliberately destructive without cause. You establish the work of your hands; you don't tear it down. The world is your work. Natural process is divine process. Your handiwork is like a potter's art (Job 10:8-10; Ps 119:73). But my mind is like a potter's wheel; round and round and round I go.

If science accurately describes your world, it's hard to avoid the sense that destruction is deliberate. Unless you restrain your sovereignty or constrain your foreknowledge, how are we to understand a love that seems so lacking in compassion? If matter and energy and space and time are all interconnected entities—related by the simplistic beauty of $E=mc^2$—then past, present, and future are already determined and done. We are left to decipher and watch it unfold. But even if time does unfold, you don't. Does this then mean that everything is determined? Is there no leeway for relationship? Or is "relationship" just an anthropomorphism, an extrapolation of my creaturely wants onto a nonexistent reality? Perhaps we exist, like knowledge itself, in a hierarchy of dimensions with you inhabiting a dimension all your own, a plane of existence we can't penetrate. As creatures, we only experience creation in creaturely fashion. My perspective is limited to my own and to what I imagine yours to be. I can't take your perspective. The finite can't inhabit the infinite, nor can the temporal inhabit the eternal. Maybe my questions *are* in vain.

I read my Bible and I perceive your world, but the connection between the two isn't always as clear as I need it to be. I know you're not the world. The Creator isn't the creation. To observe nature is not to see you. Science sees what can be seen, but as the invisible God (1 Tim 1:17) you defy such an approach. True, you revealed yourself to the ancients who wrote it as Scripture, but their report is much more poetic than pedantic. Indeed, to describe you requires the entire range of literary genre just to begin to do it justice.[9] You invite me to pray, to seek and I will find (Luke 11:9). Yet I seek and do not always find. I ask and you don't answer. Granted, I may seek what can't be found. I may ask questions for which there are no answers. I concede that in your infinite wisdom, you may simply decide to do things differently than I want. But you do say that I will find you when I seek you with all my heart (Jer 29:13). You promise that the pure in heart "will see God" (Matt 5:8).

Maybe my search isn't wholehearted. Surely it's the case that my heart isn't pure. But it's also true that I can't fathom the things science shows. I don't fully understand the Scriptures I read, either. You tell me that my hope in you cannot disappoint me, because it comes from your spirit, a guarantee of what you have promised (Rom 5:5). I just hope your promise is for more than just that which happens after I die.

I know that I won't live long. Life is a fleeting breath, a puff of air (Eccl 9:9) and not worth comparing to the glory that will be revealed (Rom 8:18). What will that glory be like? How will I experience it? Will I be *me* in eternal life?[10] Science supposes that each person exists as a single entity and substance—one physical body.[11] While I imagine myself as myself, Scripture promises that I'll be changed (1 Cor 15:51). What about the material from which I'm made? What about the dust when it returns to the dust? Cognitive science and neuroscience have closed the circle, in a sense, suggesting that the human mind (and soul) is made of the same material as the body. Whatever we know of the soul is certainly tied to the brain. Is the "real me" my brain? My brain's constantly changing already, through the effects of wear and tear, even from eating and drinking.[12]

Evolutionary biology and genetics have demonstrated our continuity with the rest of organic life. If science is right, then you created us as indivisible persons. We die as whole persons and we'll rise as whole persons. You'll clothe our mortality with immortality (1 Cor 15:53). But how does that happen? My body goes back to the dust. Who's the me that rises if I'm gone? Who is the me who inherits eternal life?

Death's still a mystery. You call it the last enemy to be destroyed (1 Cor 15:26), but it pervades all that exists. In fact, everything that exists couldn't exist apart from death. But why? If I'm a whole person crafted by your evolutionary hand, filled with your spirit and destined to experience eternity as I am, then why must I die to get there? Why not clothe my mortality beforehand? Is death actually a *natural* part of life, a created aspect of your will, a component of your own character? Maybe I should distinguish between death within you and death apart from you. Is there a difference between evolutionary death and moral death, so-called natural death and death due to sin? Finitude is a component of my creatureliness; I know I'm not immortal yet. But has creatureliness *always* presumed mortality? Would Adam have died without sin, as did his predecessors?

The question is moot. Even if death is a part of the cycle of life, my death, like Adam's, is tied to my defiant will. I refuse to be the person that you made me to be. But you love me anyway. Your grace forgives me. You died and rose to make it this way. Your death only reinterprets mine. But I'm not sure this is what I want. What I want is for you to extend my life on this earth and prevent my demise. I want you to guard me from suffering and give me a life free from pain. I want you to rescue me from death, to erase it from the human experience and to find another way. But this is not how you operate. You deal with my death by resurrecting me from it. You raise life out of loss, wring immortality out of mortality, and siphon hope out of despair.

Such is the pattern of your creation and new creation. Only through dying and rising can I move from the finite to the infinite and participate in that eternity where moments are no longer sequential but unified, where the future knows no distinction from the present.[13] In the meantime I hope for new creation, while my old creation remains the body I inhabit. My faith teaches me to trust in the fulfillment of your promises. You *have* begun a good work and will bring it to completion (Phil 1:6). My hope is based on you and not in any human potential or wishful thinking. Hope in you refuses to naively minimize life's tragedies and troubles with dismissive assurances. You see the effects of evil and sin for what they are, but then you translate them into what they *really* are. I remember Job and Paul. I remember my Lord, your Son Jesus Christ, through whom power is made perfect through weakness (2 Cor 12:9), through whom loss is the way to life. Perhaps you are the God who kills *in order* to make alive, who brings down to the grave *in order* to raise up, who makes poor *in order* to make rich, who humbles *in order* to exalt.

This makes some sense of hardships that are circumstances of human life but not human cause. The cross translates suffering into meaningful redemption and reinforced character, rather than leaving it as meaningless pain or just desserts. Instead of a simple end to be feared, death becomes the gateway to life.

Yet even as I pray all of these things, my mind feels like I'm forcing a fit. Science reveals a world where randomness seems the norm, death is constant and the future is open-ended. How do I reconcile this? How do I make sense of what makes no sense? If all truth is your truth, how does what I believe come together with what nature reveals? How do I deal with this dissonance?

I have options. You are the potter and I am the clay pot, a broken, leaky clay pot at that. Who am I to question you? Where was I when you laid the earth's foundation? Have I ever given orders to the morning, or shown the dawn its place (Job 38 4, 12)? Maybe I should be silent.

I could choose to adjust my categories. As God you are good, just, and competent; but maybe goodness, justice, and competence from your vantage point dramatically diverge from how I understand them. Maybe up is down and right is wrong.

I could lower my expectations. Your letting be is a letting go. You let us loose to figure out life for ourselves, refusing to intervene because of the high value you place on creation's freedom.

There is a final option. It could be that my faith is in vain, and that it's only some evolutionary aberration or survival mechanism. The reason you seem so detached and absent is because you are. Maybe you don't exist.

But none of these options seems legitimate. Even if I am a metaphorical clay pot, I'm still only one *metaphorically*. You don't craft in your image inanimate objects but rather personal beings, endowed with your Spirit and character for personal relationships with you. Adjusting categories isn't an option either. Questions about your goodness, justice, and competence can't be silenced by appealing to the infinite distance between creature and Creator. Our ideas of justice and goodness may be flawed approximations, but they still derive from the ideal that ultimately resides with you. Otherwise they're meaningless. As far as lowering expectations goes, that may ease my disappointment, but what I'm left with is a pretty tepid faith that's hardly worth having. I guess I could just give up, lose hope, get cynical. But that doesn't alleviate the dissonance either.

"Lord, you have been our dwelling place throughout all generations. Before the mountains were born or you brought forth the earth and the world, from everlasting to everlasting you are God" (Ps 90:1-2 NIV). I will deal with the dissonance by standing firm in my faith. I will seek you with my whole heart. I will persist in my prayer.

CHAPTER 7

SUNDAY LUNCH

I thought we'd never eat," Dave said as we walked over to Aunt Bernice's house one Sunday after church. Aunt Bernice likes to meet my friends and always says that the primary rehearsal for the glories of heaven's wedding banquet is not a fancy cocktail party, a Saturday picnic, or the swankiest of dinner soirees. No, she says that the only suitable dress rehearsal for the banquet table of God is Sunday lunch.[1]

"Having feasted upon the word of God in worship, we now feast with great thanksgiving upon the provisions of God set before us at this table." Aunt Bernice could get a little dramatic. But then again, so could we. It was easy to get effusive over Aunt Bernice's fried chicken. I hope they serve it in heaven.

"Did you know that the chicken is the closest living relative of the *Tyrannosaurus rex*?"[2] I couldn't resist.

"Good heavens, honey, are you still thinking about evolution?" Aunt Bernice wasn't sure she liked the idea of eating fried dinosaur-cousin.

"I've been praying about it too," I replied.

"Well, anything that gets you talking to God can't be all bad," she sighed.

"Tell me this," Dave said as he reached for the dill-hinted potato salad (another heavenly necessity), "if God endowed creation with potential and guides it toward a purposeful end, what's up with mosquitoes?" Dave likes to hike, but he hates the bugs. "Someone fell asleep at *that* gene mutation switch."

Either that or mosquitoes are an example of what happens when nature is free. How else to explain a blood-sucking pest whose only benefit to the ecosystem seems to be as junk food for fish and bats (no way Noah would have let them onto the ark if he could have helped it)? Creation's freedom is part of God's plan, but to grant freedom means permitting the things freedom produces.

I could say that mosquitoes are a consequence of Adam's fall, and in a sense they are. Current research pegs the emergence of mosquitoes in the late Neolithic period (before 4000 B.C.).[3] This means they emerge at the same time as the irresistible population surge of pre-*Homo sapiens* humans, making mosquitoes ripe for infiltrating creation once Adam gets booted from the garden. Scientists argue that mosquitoes benefit the ecosystem by controlling vertebrate populations, humans included, that would otherwise overly reproduce.[4] But maybe I'm stretching it here.

It is the case, however, that the earth is tied to the choices humans make once they show up on the scene. It's what the Bible describes as *dominion* (Gen 1:26), the responsibility for creation that comes with being made in God's image. But again the sad story of humanity's dominion is our insistence on exercising *domination* instead. Rather than care for creation, a paradisiac harmony depicted as Eden, we opted for control, which got us expelled from Eden and placed at odds with creation. Theology calls this the "curse of the fall," the fall*out* of human sin (3:1-19).

How is it that people made in God's image to act as God acts could make such bad choices? Was God's competent creativity not quite up to snuff? Did he fail to work out the bugs?

Free Will and Its Limits

The "freewill defense" that theologians use to account for human sin extends to the entire realm of nature. Remember, the freewill defense begins with God desiring a personal relationship with persons made in his image.[5] But in order for such a relationship to be genuine, God cannot force it. Coerced love is not love. Thus God factors free will into the system for the sake of relationship. Allowing freedom to love means there exists freedom to reject love. Ergo the rub. In order to have genuine relationships with people, God must permit the possibility of *no* relationship.

Take this theo-logic and extrapolate it to nature as a whole and you have what is called the "free process defense."[6] God doesn't desire a personal relationship with creation the way that he does with people, but God's own relational nature can't help but show up in nature. God himself exists in eternal relationship: Father, Son, and Holy Spirit. Each person of the Trinity delights in the other, freely loving and receiving love, submitting to one another for love's sake. If evolution is the handiwork of God, then we would expect it to function as it does, with the same sort of freedom we experience as humans (as chess novices playing with the Grand Master). It makes sense that the freedom we experience results from the free process God employed to make us. A free-process creation results in free-willed people. But just as the *free will* of people can result in rejecting God's will, so the *free process* of creation results in mosquitoes and the diseases they carry—not to mention genetic deformities, hurricanes, and earthquakes, all outcomes of a creation that is free to become what it will become.

"The problem with that whole line of defense is that it makes God seem like his hands are tied," Dave said, the *T. rex* gravy dribbling off his chin. "Once he grants freedom of process, he has to sit back and let it roll."

"Don't talk with your mouth full," Aunt Bernice scolded. "And don't tell me God has his hands tied, either. If you're looking to blame somebody for the mess in this world, blame the devil."

Personally, I struggle with blaming the devil for what's wrong with the world. It seems as if most misery in our world can find sufficient attribution in our own human depravity. Yet at the same time, I'm also aware that there is evil that surpasses the accumulation of individual transgressions. Call it cosmic evil or systemic sin, it's the kind of sinister corruption that results in the horrors of holocausts, world wars, ecological upheaval, global poverty, and ecclesial abuses. For such endemic evil, Satan is a viable suspect. Still, if the Bible teaches us anything, it teaches us that any satanic power we confront on earth is already a defeated power—no matter how contrary it may seem to our experience (Rev 20:10).

When it comes to disease and disaster, I prefer the idea of a fallen creation—that somehow our succumbing to Satan's enticements fueled the chaos we experience as disease and disaster, especially given the biblical connections between human sin and creation's decay (Gen 3:17; Rom 8:21-22). But diseases and disasters occurred long before Adam bit off more than he could chew, long before *Homo sapiens* showed up at all. It really doesn't work to say that diseases and disasters are outcomes of a fallen creation. They're the outcomes of a competent yet free creation, a creation that operates the way God made it.

Human freedom and creation's freedom often clash. But the clash is usually due to human choice. You can't blame God when you build your house too close to the shore or along a known geologic fault line. You can pray that God might redirect the weather or stabilize tectonic plates, but to be realistic, living in God's world is more about conforming to its limits than expecting God to conform to human demands. Still, I would like to think that God would do more to guard his people from harm. Earthquakes and tsunamis kill thousands. Is this an unavoidable outcome of freedom? The unavoidable consequence of human choices? Does God value freedom so much as to be constrained by it?

"I told you I'll not have any of that tied-up God talk at my dinner table. Especially on Sunday." Aunt Bernice tightened her grip on her wooden spoon.

Frankly, there are too many places in the Bible where God defies creaturely freedom to suggest that his hands are ever tied. However, in most of those places, God's defiance of creaturely freedom is in response to human *abuses* of freedom, such as when disease, weather, or earthquakes are employed as agents of divine judgment (e.g., Exod 9:3; 1 Kgs 17:1; Isa 29:6). The same is true with regard to redemption. God defies creaturely freedom in response to human abuses of freedom by dying on the cross and rising from the dead. However, there are other places where bad things *just happen*. God's response there is to suggest that you consider it as incentive to get your life in order (Luke 13:1-5).

If God is a competent creator, we have to view natural phenomena as exhibitions of his competence—and as far as earthquakes and hurricanes go, exhibitions of his majesty (Isa 29:6 and elsewhere). God's involvement is miraculous at times, though miracles remain the exception rather than the rule. If miracles were normal, we couldn't call them *miraculous*. Miracles show up at special intersections in biblical history as exclamation points to stress the purposes and identity of God. God need not miraculously intervene to be involved in his creation. To love sometimes means to let things be. For God to so love the world may mean a refusal to flout his own craftsmanship or to violate the character of relationship.[7] God curbs his omnipotence, if you will, for love's sake.

For God to limit his omnipotence is not far-fetched. Look no further than the incarnation. By taking on human flesh in Christ, God automatically sets boundaries on two classic characteristics of divinity. As human, God in Christ is no longer omnipresent (everywhere at once). And as human, God in Christ is no longer omniscient (knowing everything at once; Mark 13:32). But even without the incarnation, omnipotence still has its limits. Clearly God cannot sin, but neither can God contradict himself. Thomas Aquinas rightly asserted that "whatever implies contradiction does not come within the scope of divine omnipotence" (*Summa theolog-ica* 1.25.3). "You may attribute miracles to God," C. S. Lewis concurred, "but not nonsense."[8]

"Speaking of nonsense—," Aunt Bernice was already getting wary.

As far as we can tell, the freedom God bestows on creation takes the shape of the open-endedness and flexibility science witnesses within the evolutionary process. It is creation's freedom of *process* (evolution) which results in the freedom of *persons*, all brought about by God.[9] Yet the freedom of process that evolution displays is not without its own drawbacks. True, as the handiwork of a competent Creator, the complexity and beauty that has emerged over the eons testifies to the creativity of free process. Yet the beauty and wonder of the universe has come at great cost. Evolution has required billions of years of apparent waste and futility. The entire epic of species survival is wrought with what is often viewed as a cruel struggle for survival.[10] And all of this before human sin shows up to exacerbate things. Death is the price biological emergence must pay.[11] Is the cost too great? Depends on your perspective. Only if one organism dies can another generation emerge. Biological death, whether to serve natural selection or to provide food and energy for survival, is an evolutionary necessity.

"But doesn't the Bible say that death entered the world through the sin of Adam (Rom 5:12), and that it is the last enemy to be destroyed (1 Cor 15:26)?" Dave is one of the more popular Sunday school teachers. He's in charge of the middle school students, which makes him even more popular (with the adults).

Yes, the Bible does say that. But the death the Bible describes is specif-ically human death, not organic death in general.[12] Check the fossils. Organisms have died ever since they emerged and throughout the course of evolution. Death has occurred since the first breath of biological life (and some would say since the first "breath" of cosmological life), long before Adam inhaled. Ironically, therefore, death must be another part of God's good creation. But as with the resurrection, the overarching outcome of evolutionary death is not the destruction of life, but its sustenance and flourishing.[13]

To accept death as essential to biological life is easier if you view natural selection as a positive process whereby the negativity of death is redeemed for the sake of new life.[14] Look at it this way and, again, you're able to see in evolution a preview of the way God will act to redeem the negativity of death due to sin. Jesus said, "Unless a kernel of wheat falls to the ground and dies, it remains only a single seed. But if it dies, it produces many seeds" (John 12:24 NIV). More than stating the horticulturally obvious, Jesus makes a much larger point about the way all things are. Just as the death of an organism will allow for its flourishing reproduction and continued genetic life (not that the Bible would put it this way), so would the death of Jesus and the subsequent deaths of Jesus' followers lead to a new flourishing and continuation of life. In God, death is redeemed for good.

But enough with the apologetic. Trying to explain God's work can start to look arrogant if you go on for too many pages.

"Amen to that," Aunt Bernice interjected. It was almost time for peach pie.

Body and Soul

Christianity has always held that God's ways resist our ability to fully comprehend them (Isa 64:4; 1 Cor 2:9). What exists as most *real* is at the same time most *hidden* from view (2 Cor 4:18), though I still prefer the word *mysterious* (from the Greek meaning "hidden"). There's plenty of mystery in science, be it in the mysteries of quantum indeterminacy or the mysteries of human consciousness. We walk by faith and not by sight at many levels. But both theologically *and* scientifically speaking, an inability to comprehend does not imply nonexistence. We still can't hear that dog whistle. We cannot see God.

As limited creatures with limited brains, we're kind of like comic strip characters existing in two-dimensional space. We see spheres, but only comprehend them as circles. We can only function from left to right (if we're functioning in English). But like the comic strip reader, God sees reality as it fully exists; he sees the past and the future all at once. God reads us like a comic strip—one that he's drawn with his own pen (and one that must make him laugh some mornings). Yet even in our comic-strip existence, while we can't comprehend everything, we can comprehend the things God reveals. And science provides a powerful lens. Science helps us see nature's complexity and elegance, and faith then helps us see the complexity and elegance of nature as *creation*.[15] Having two lenses is a good thing (one for each eye). Aunt Bernice will look at a sunset and praise the Lord, even though she understands the physics. That's how faith and science see together.

Aunt Bernice agreed, "As short wavelength blues and greens of sunlight are scattered at dusk, the remaining longer wavelengths that reach my eyes *are* beautiful, especially when reflected by dust particles or water."

Wow. Aunt Bernice sure picked up physics fast.

Not to be outdone, I added, "If science has it right, then my ability to have faith and use science together is because my brain functions as it does. My neural capacities, specifically my ability to use language and be conscious of myself, sets me apart from other creatures both biologically and theologically."

Dave was offended by my use of the first person singular as representative. "You're not the only one with a brain, you know."

"He does act like that sometimes, doesn't he?" Aunt Bernice remarked to everyone in the plural. "Book-learning is a fine thing, honey, but don't flaunt it."

Language and sentience emerged as our brains developed such that by the time *Homo sapiens* showed up, humans possessed the God-given capacity for personal relationship. We were able to consider the thoughts of others, remember things, control mental behavior, make decisions, and consider the future.[16] Theologically, language and consciousness correspond to word and spirit, characteristics of God (John 1:1; Rom 8:9) and rightly reflected in people made in his image. However, what ultimately makes my capacity for relationship a sacred thing is not *my* ability to have faith but *God's* willingness to relate to me. It is God personally loving me that establishes my intrinsic value and worth as a *person*.[17] As much as anything, to be a person is what distinguishes humans from the rest of the animal kingdom.

Granted, all of this capacity and consciousness has a downside. While I am able to relate, cogitate, and verbally communicate, I am also aware that I am going to die. Fear of death is a reason many people consider God in the first place. That we all will die someday is a biological and theological certainty. The problem evolution presents is the question, *what keeps going after I'm gone?* If believing in Jesus gets me eternal life, how does that happen?

Evolutionary biology and neuroscience dispute any Cartesian[18] dichotomy between soul and body, a heretofore helpful distinction that would have allowed for my *person* to transcend my physical body into eternity even while my material shell decomposed. Though many Christians embrace the concept of an immortal soul, Christianity proper has traditionally affirmed the resurrection of the *body* instead of a separation of body and soul at death (see the Apostles' Creed). However, we know that the resurrected body can't be the exact same bodies we currently inhabit. Our bodies decompose in the ground once we die. So what does "resurrection of the body" mean? If my personality is housed in my physical body and brain,[19] and if there is no disembodied soul, then how does my identity survive into eternity? In what way will I be *me* when I'm dead?

Paul describes the resurrection body as a *spiritual* body (1 Cor 15:44), but given Jesus' own resurrected appearance as a flesh and blood person (Luke 24:39), there's no warrant for thinking that *spiritual* means *nonphysical*. Sure, Paul draws the distinction between *natural* and spiritual, but the distinction should probably be read as the distinction we make between a *corpse* (a buried body or what Paul calls a *sown* body—think back to that seed of wheat in the ground) and a *living* body (that is, a *raised* or resurrected body). There's also no warrant to thinking our bodies will be so completely different as to be unrecognizable. We will be living bodies in some way as we now are, having evolved not as containers for souls but as whole persons.

"Are you telling me I'm stuck with these hips for eternity?" Aunt Bernice had been counting on not having to do Weight Watchers in heaven.

The point is that you will be *you* to the extent that others will know you. Those who saw the risen Jesus recognized him (eventually). Therefore, the person I am in heaven somehow includes the body I am, even if it's not the same body I am. We can quibble and dream over what our bodies will be like—free from pain and disease for sure, and maybe even unwanted cellulite, baldness, and the aches of aging—but theology and biology both insist on *physical* bodies. We're physical people on earth and we'll be physical people in heaven like Christ (1 Cor 15:20-23). As redeemed creatures in a redeemed creation, there is continuity between here and there.

While we are our bodies, it is the case that unlike Jesus, we will not be the same bodies we presently are. (Biologically, we're not even the bodies we were last year.) Unlike Jesus, we're sinful creatures whose sin has infected our dying such that at death our bodies (our selves) decay as Jesus' body did not. He left the tomb intact (albeit with scars), while we'll require some refashioning. God has to purge the sin out of our system and make our bodies like Christ's (Phil 3:21). Therefore my eternal embodiment, while continuous with my current self, is not the same as my current body.

"Then I think I'll have another scoop of ice cream on my pie," Aunt Bernice smiled.

In Heaven as It Isn't on Earth

"Paul did say 'We will be changed' (1 Cor 15:52)," Dave added, his middle-school Sunday-school preparations impressive.

Whatever the physical resurrection of the body looks like, the change will likely be into something that exists outside the space-time environment we currently inhabit.[20] We'll have to step outside the comic strip. Eternal life is life outside the creaturely boundaries of physics and biology where death and time play pivotal roles and do their deleterious deeds. But how do I get from here to there? What happens in the meantime? Where am I if "I" am rotting in the ground on my way back to the dust from whence I came (Gen 3:19)? Do I say that my self remains in God's memory, so that when it is time for new creation to arrive he "remembers" me back into my new self?[21] Is this what it means to reside "in Christ"? Does the redemption/new creation of the earth somehow reconstitute the bodies buried or cremated in it? Or does my "self" temporarily separate from my body until I get my new body?

Given the language of creation, we would expect new creation to bear plenty of similarities to life on earth now (at least all the good stuff). For God to pronounce creation "very good" would imply that it's worth redeeming. The biggest difference will be the eternality of the new. Because death is a natural component of nature and evolution, everything on earth has always been destined to die, including humans. For Adam to have been formed from the dust of the ground (2:7) binds him to all biological life that likewise was formed from the ground (2:9, 19).[22] The implication, then, is that Adam would have died on earth like every other creature, even if he had never sinned.[23] Even those who inherit eternal life through faith in Jesus Christ die. Eternal life has never been about living forever on this earth. This earth was never made to be heaven. Adam's sin infects death with its existential horror and ruptures our relationship with God. But in the end, whether you believe in Jesus or not, you still go back to the dirt.

Paul does write that death entered the world through Adam (Rom 5:12). But again, if evolution is the way God works, then perhaps what Paul meant by death was not the inevitable cessation of life on this earth but rather the eternal death of a relationship with God for those who have no faith in Christ (John 3:18).

"But didn't God say to Adam: 'of the tree of the knowledge of good and evil you shall not eat, for in the day that you eat of it you shall die' (Gen 2:17)? That surely seems to indicate that had Adam behaved himself he could have avoided pushing up daisies." Dave's level of Bible acumen might be wasted on his middle-schoolers.

Read Genesis again and you'll see that Adam and Eve ate but didn't drop dead at the foot of the tree afterward. They got kicked out of the garden, yes, but they were still breathing on their way out the gate. Again, it could be that the Bible is making a distinction between biological death and the death humans suffer as eternal alienation from God.

If Adam had lived "forever," eventually (5 billion years from now) the sun would still run out of hydrogen, burn out, blow up, and take the earth with it. Adam and Eve, though very old, would be very dead. But actually, there's no need to insist that Adam and Eve would have lived forever on this earth.[24] Even Jesus aged. If Adam's life on this earth had been a sin-free paradise, it still could not have been *eternal.* Physics as we understand it could not allow earth to go on indefinitely. If we understand physics rightly, then God never intended earth to go on indefinitely either (since God is the author of physics). Eternal life is not about living forever on this planet. It's about a relationship with God that transcends this world into new creation.

CHAPTER 8

PEACH PIE IN THE SKY

Evil and Adam's Fall

Go back to the bigger question of how a 'very good' creature, made in the image of God, would ever abuse his freedom to begin with. Sure, the serpent did the tempting, but where did *the will to sin* come from? And how did the serpent get into paradise anyway?" Dave wanted to talk a bit longer. He wasn't done eating yet.

Generally, it's been taught that as people we are *tarnished* images, but again, that seems to imply an incompetent Creator. Falling back onto the freewill defense helps to a point, but it still doesn't explain how the free choice to disobey God got chosen. I could project all sorts of psychological rationales backwards onto the first couple—like how nothing is more attractive than something that's taboo, or how the grass is always greener on the other side of the fence (which would clearly make paradise problematic). Then again there's always the possibility that Adam and Eve were dupes. But how would that ever have been very good?

"I told you to blame the devil!" Aunt Bernice inserted, waving her wooden spoon now.

Many figure that the devil's fall would have happened prior to Adam's sin, which if correct, at least explains the serpent's presence in the garden. But that doesn't explain the first couple's succumbing to the serpent's wiles. What was there in original human nature that would have fed any willingness to defy God? Biologically speaking, does our evolutionary past in any way contribute to our proclivity to sin? Natural selection does promote self-preservation, which could certainly give way to selfishness. Natural selection also rewards aggression for the sake of survival. It's not hard to imagine how the will to survive could distort any will to obey. Natural selection is not a bad thing by itself. There's nothing morally wrong with hunting for food or caring for your kin or adjusting to your environment. Evolutionary behaviors would not be considered evil in and of themselves, since their purpose is to benefit life and growth.

St. Augustine, the great fifth-century church father and philosopher, taught that evil derives its existence and energy from the goodness it perverts. Evil has no essential being of its own. Thus, aspects of evolution created by God as good (such as the survival instinct) deviously warp to suit ulterior purposes. The self-interest that serves to benefit life deforms into the self-obsession that debases life. That our biological makeup can be bent toward self-obsession and violence suggests that the notorious notion of original sin may be even more sinister than originally thought.

The doctrine of original sin does not take you and me off the hook. To do evil remains a personal moral choice. Yet the distortion of our biological predilections could account for the capacity to choose evil in the first place. Freedom becomes corrupted through exposure to temptation. Satan's enticement fueled Eve's twisted logic ("the woman saw that the fruit of the tree was good for food"; Gen 3:6 NIV). The wrong choice suddenly made sense. This infected free will propagates into the exponentially more radical evil that defines human history. Beginning with Cain's slaughter of Abel and cascading into the heinous acts of humanity against humanity, the spiral of evil has spun out of control. As creatures made in God's image, we possess the potential for the most radical of evil, much of which has been exhibited horrifically over the course of human history.

Because of the interrelatedness of creatures and creation, as well as our role as creation's stewards (Gen 1:28), our sinful choices impair creation's own ability to thrive.[3] For evidence look no further than the ominous forecasts of global warming and the environmental effects of suburban sprawl. In Genesis 2, there's a lack of vegetation because God had yet to send rain and people to work the ground (2:5). Human beings, as bearers of God's image, are also sharers of his creative work. The earth is dependent on us in ways that we're just now coming to appreciate, albeit hazardously. We're discovering that we can't use the resources the earth provides as we please. Dominion is not domination; the effects of sin are not purely metaphysical, nor are they confined to human tragedy. The creation groans, Paul writes (Rom 8:22), eager to be let out from under the weight. Evil is systemic as much as it is individualistic.

"You know," Dave added, "my middle schoolers all say that the biggest obstacle to their believing in God is the 'problem of evil.' If God is great and God is good, why do bad things happen?"

Surprisingly, when you trace back through Christian history, you rarely find evil addressed as a "problem," that is, a puzzle to be solved or a question to be answered.[4] The reason is that evil eludes reason. Evil makes no sense. Its incomprehensibility extends beyond the problematic. Its illogic is part of what makes evil so evil. Evil defies understanding. Augustine said that to explain evil is like trying to "see darkness" or "hear silence" (*De civitate Dei* 12.7). Even if you blame the devil, what made the devil decide to become the devil? Augustine described evil as basically the absence of good, that it is essentially *nonbeing*. If evil doesn't exist (but is anti-existence), it can't be a problem. Yet because there is evil, we're left to acknowledge its anti-existence as a kind of existence, which only compounds its perversity. And it is this very perversity that corrupts our God-given freedom, not only to cause us to choose wrong but to make us responsible for choosing wrong.[5]

"But if I understand you right, evolutionary theory has nothing to say about evil just as it has nothing to say about God," Dave said, understanding me right.

"Yes, dear, but that's because evolution is evil," Aunt Bernice smirked. She was trying to bait me. I have this vein that pops up in the center of my forehead when I get too intense. My family takes turns trying to make it show itself.

It's not until the capacity for relationship emerges in *Homo sapiens* that evil can be spoken of in any substantive sense (if you're willing to concede death as a biological necessity). There is no morality where there is no personal choice (even if we label creation as a free *process*, there's no free choice as with human free will). Through Adam sinful death enters the world, that is, death that separates us from God in a way that death was never intended to do. As evil perverts goodness, so sin loads death with its curse. For Adam to die without sin presumes that, like Christ, he would have enjoyed the fellowship of God in eternal life after he died (glorified body and all). But once he sinned, he became dependent on the cross for that life. Christianity teaches that the senselessness of evil is met by the foolishness of the cross (1 Cor 1:18). God eradicates evil by subjecting himself to it. Turning the tables on evil, the cross subverts the power of the evil it conquers (Mark 10:45). It doesn't address the issue of evil's origins, but it is an answer to evil's existence.

Time

However, the cross as the answer to evil does raise another interesting question with regard to evolution. If God's intention was never eternal life enjoyed on the earth as it is now (which it couldn't have been with the universe existing as it does), then perhaps creation is not so much something good that went bad but something started as good that just is not yet done. It's as if redemption was the purpose from the beginning. It's as if the creation is being pulled, *called* toward that day when all things become radically new in Christ.[6] If perfection never was and is "not-yet," the appearance of evil and suffering (including the suffering and struggle depicted by Darwinian science) is no longer inconceivable. That the serpent got into the garden may suggest that everything was not yet right with the world, even before everything went wrong.[7]

You definitely see this in regard to human beings. Adam was never supposed to exist as the epitome of humanity. That designation belongs to Jesus, "the last Adam" (1 Cor 15:45).[8] Jesus was not some contingency plan "just in case" Adam blew it. Knowing *free will* would end up as *free won't* (but allowing it nonetheless for the sake of genuine relationship), God accounts for human freedom through his own free and voluntary sacrifice of himself. "Greater love has no one than this," Jesus said, "that [someone] lay down his life for his friends" (John 15:13 NIV). Redemption was the plan from the start. Adam and Eve lived as *only* human (a phrase I often use to excuse my own poor behavior), but Jesus lived as *truly* human. Christ redeems us, not *from* our humanity, but into our *true* humanity. The humanity of Jesus is what God intended from the beginning but what creation (on its own) was never made to produce. Creation has always been aimed toward new creation, the final redemption of all things in Christ (Rom 8:19-21).

What this entails is that you flip your Bible around and read the end as the beginning. Instead of Genesis, what if Revelation is the more plausible place from which to view God's creative design? What if the new heaven and new earth (Rev 21:1) already exist in eternity, and we're just waiting for our experience to catch up with that reality—a compression, if you will, of eternity and time.[9] Eschatology, literally the study of "last things," is really the study of *matchless* things, those things that comprise the ultimate reality of God. As ultimate reality, these matchless things are things that exist *before* the beginning as well as after the end.[10] What God created was good, just not yet finished; partial, just not yet complete. Evolution is not the means whereby this completion occurs. It is the eventual unveiling of ultimate reality. Nobody believes the world will *evolve* toward perfection. That is, evolution is not the means whereby all things are made new (21:5). New creation is an extra-natural singularity. But the fact that evolution can be viewed as *progressive* suggests that there is an end toward which things are being lured.

God always finishes what he starts, which is how Scripture can speak of new creation as having already happened. "I *saw* a new heaven and a new earth," John writes in Rev 21, "the first heaven and the first earth had passed away" (21:1, italics mine). The tree of life planted in the garden is not chipped into mulch on account of Adam's sin, but exists and thrives in the true paradise of God, awaiting humanity's ultimate salvation into true humanity and image-bearing (22:2).[11] Death is required (2 Cor 5:17). In one of the most sublime of all paradoxes, the cross ends up not as the instrument of execution it was designed for, but as the tree of life whereby Jesus completes Adam's (and therefore our) faithfulness. Death becomes the gateway to eternal life it was supposed to be in the first place—foreshadowed by evolution's own use of death as the gateway to biological new life.

"You know," Dave added, a little worried this time, "there's still the problem of God knowing evil is coming but not doing something to stop it."

"I don't like that," Aunt Bernice snapped.

Some theologians would prefer to confine God to time and somehow disassociate him from the occurrence of death and evil, asserting that God can't know the future since the future does not yet exist in the present. This notion has come to be known as "open theology."[12] While not as problematic as "process theology" (wherein God himself evolves over time), confining God's knowledge to the boundaries of time too severely cuts into essential characteristics of God, namely his timelessness and omniscience. To situate God in time makes him subject to it, rather than the Creator of it. And while God does subject himself to the limits of time with the incarnation, it's a temporary arrangement for a special purpose.

While we do experience time as a constant tick-tock flow from future to past,[13] Albert Einstein challenged the idea of time as a constant, fundamental reality. He showed that time, as we experience it, is to a significant extent an illusion (which has become a great excuse for me when I'm late).[14] As an alternative to the idea of *flowing time*, some physicists argue for what is called a *block universe*, meaning that everything exists in the conceptual present, whether we view things as past, present, or future (like the comic strip reader reading the comics).[15] Unbound by time, God sits in this block universe and reads all events of history simultaneously. The problem with this idea is that it places the "problem" of evil back in God's lap, the very thing open and process theology seek to work around by constraining God to time.

However, Scripture asserts that God both knows the future and acts within history to shape the future (e.g. Isa 46:10; Jer 29:11). Physics supports this capacity for doing so. As an object approaches the speed of light, it gets more and more massive and thus requires more and more energy to speed it up. Consequently, the object never reaches light speed because by then its mass would have to be infinite and it would take an infinite amount of energy to get it there (sorry, *Star Wars* fans). The only thing that can move at the speed of light is light itself.[16] When the Bible declares that God is light (1 John 1:5), it may be saying more about God than that he exists as pure goodness. From a physics standpoint, to be light is to be infinite. By way of analogy, if you imagine God as light hanging out at the speed of light (which is what light does), then this means that no time passes for God, even as the entirety of universal history passes for the rest of the cosmos. God illumines all of history at once, even as the objects of history are limited by their finitude.[17] The future does not fade into the past but exists as eternally present.

"Dude, are you just messing with us now?" Dave wasn't one to get too ethereal.

In the final analysis, physics and theology still leave evil and death in God's lap. And frankly, I'd rather leave them there than anywhere else. For those bothered by God's knowing something without doing something about it, the physics of light would suggest that to *know* would not mean to *be able* to do. Just as time-bound objects cannot approach light-speed without expanding into infinity, so God does not enter into time without being bound by time. His own creative work places boundaries on his own divine involvement. God knows, but is not able to do anything he wants, limited as he is by curbs he imposes on his own omnipotence. As hard as this is to conceive, we have to accept the creation as a total package, an all-or-nothing arrangement whereby you have to take the good with the bad.[8]

"What's time got to do with evolution?" Aunt Bernice prefers to stay on topic.

The vastness of time is a key component of evolution. Darwin knew he was done without it because his theory required the universe to be very old in order for evolution to occur. And why the vastness theologically? It gives us a glimpse of the vastness of God, especially when we recognize it as characteristic of God. Not only is God eternal, but he has all the time in the world.

"Speaking of time," Dave said, rubbing his stomach, "I gotta be going. Good thing, if I stay here I'll just keep eating and you'll have to put me out of my misery whether or not death is characteristic of God too."

The Last Enemy or Necessary Companion?

Death, as both endemic and essential to the evolutionary epic, suggests death-as-sacrificial-giving to be a core characteristic of God. Jesus said that the greatest love you can show is to lay down your life for another (John 15:13), which he then exhibited by laying down his own life for sinners (Rom 5:8). Christianity holds up the cross as the supreme demonstration of sacrificial love, but might it not also be that the entire creation demonstrates God's sacrificial character? Evolution operates through the continual death of one generation for the sake of the next, displaying what could be described as a cross-shaped creation. Sacrificial giving is part of God's nature and thus part of nature.[19] Evolution reveals God's inimitable generosity, both in lavishing the universe with creative potential as well as in weaving sacrifice into its processes.

"But isn't it too much of a stretch to interpret 'survival of the fittest' as sacrificial giving? Since when does competing for resources and predation denote altruism?" Dave never was much for euphemisms. "Show me one mosquito that's ever bitten me for unselfish reasons!"

Remember that much of what gets attributed to the behavior of organisms is a projection of human behavior. As proponents of a more symbiotic view of evolution would argue, what looks like competition could also be seen as cooperation. Even with the mosquito infecting the mammal, there's still a greater good that may be at work if a balanced ecosystem is of high value (not that I'm personally changing my mind about mosquitoes, either). What happens with evolution is that a species adapts to its environment for the sake of being fruitful and multiplying. Whether this is interpreted as selfish or sacrificial really depends on your point of view. A bacterium cannot be selfish any more than a fungus can be sacrificial in and of itself. It is a theology of nature that provides the interpretive lens.

To view nature as a creation is a theological move, as is viewing creation as the manifestation of God's character. We see with the eyes of faith. As for God's self-sacrificial generosity in creation, it should not be seen as something God does uncharacteristically or because the situation demanded it. God's love, freedom, generosity, and self-sacrifice *is* God. God loves because he must; he creates because he must; he gives because he must; he redeems because he must—God must be God.[20] And thus we expect to see the marks of God on the world as science observes it even if science doesn't acknowledge it. God gives himself in creation and for creation, ultimately dying to redeem it toward new creation. Though it is important to remember that any self-sacrifice on God's part does not imply an *inherent* limitation of God's power.[21] God *chooses* to limit himself of his own free will. If anything, sacrifice bears witness to God's *paradoxical* power, the very power that is "made perfect in weakness" (2 Cor 12:9). And not only his power but his goodness too. Because God's goodness often comes shaped as a cross (whether in creation or in redemption), it may not always *feel* good or even *look* good. Yet because it is cross-shaped, it's purposes are *for* good every time. Death is necessary for life to evolve and death is necessary for life to be redeemed into eternal life. It's the necessity of death in the handiwork of God that so strongly argues for the presence of sacrificial death within the character of God.

John the Baptist identifies Jesus as the "Lamb of God who takes away the sin of the world" (John 1:29). There the reference seems to be an allusion to Isaiah 53, where the coming redeemer is described as "a lamb that is led to the slaughter" (53:7). In Revelation, the same terminology is used to describe Christ in terms that stretch even further back: "the Lamb *[having been]* slain from the creation of the world" (Rev 13:8 NIV, italics mine). While the placement of the modifier "from the creation of the world" is debated, to read this verse as indicating the intentionality of God to redeem his creation in Christ from the very beginning is not so much of a stretch (see Eph 1:4-5). This advances the idea that evolutionary death as a part of creation foreshadows Christ's redemptive work—a redemption that was always in the works, both for the creature and the creation (Rom 8:20). Evolution itself testifies to the redemption of Christ!

"You been drinking my cooking sherry." Aunt Bernice still wasn't totally persuaded.

As theologian Jürgen Moltmann reminds, God's "resolve to create also means a resolve to save."[22] Through Christ, *death* is translated as *victory*, whether the outcome be advanced biological life or new resurrection life. Death gives life. The evil is not in the dying but in the sinner's eternal alienation from God. Having been reconciled to God in Christ, Paul can delightfully declare not that death is gone (not yet at least) but that it has lost its sting, the sting that it procured that fateful day in the garden (1 Cor 15:55-56). Creation, which occurred with redemption in view, was set up from the get-go to withstand whatever evil got into the system, sort of like a cosmic antivirus program. God knew Adam and Eve would blow it, but their rejection of God was part of the risk of genuine relationship. Yet in the end, seen from the future, even the risk inherent in genuine relationship wasn't really a risk. Evil's moves have been checked. The devil is already defeated. The Grand Master always wins the game.

"I am making everything new," God promises (Rev 21:5 NIV), even as it is already occurring. What does new creation imply? Revelation already promises no more death (21:4). Does this include all creaturely death? Do no mosquitoes get swatted in heaven? Or do they not bite in the first place? If "no death" literally means *no death* (which it must mean if we're talking eternity), then we should anticipate a new creation with a new sort of biology and physics—at least one where entropy no longer holds sway and death is no longer required. With no death there would be no evolution, since in heaven, presumably, everything achieves its perfection. Certainly God will no longer need to limit himself in any fashion. Inasmuch as earth is modeled after heaven, approximations will cease and time will compress and defragment. We will finally experience a unity of self as whole beings in Christ—past, present, and future.[23]

Nevertheless, since God foreknew redemption's necessity before it was ever necessary, it may be that there is more of a continuity between creation and new creation than is typically believed. What God made was good, just not yet finished or perfected.[24] Ours is not a good world gone bad, even if it has been made bad by humanity's abuse. Ours is a world in waiting, a world responding to a call toward completion. Whatever is meant by our personal identity in the eschatological future, it already exists here in the present.[25] Paul writes that not only has God raised Christ and seated him by his side in heaven, but God has raised us up and seated us too (Eph 2:6). By faith in Christ your seat in heaven is already saved. But more than that, at least as far as God is concerned, you're already sitting in it! "You have been raised with Christ," Paul wrote to the Colossians (3:1), even as they still lived and breathed on earth. Instead of thinking of our existence as two components—body and soul—it's better to think of it as two aspects—first and final. Or, even better—already and not yet, both of which exist simultaneously.[26] We will become who we already are in Christ.

The same is true for the earth and new earth (or it wouldn't be called a new *earth*; Isa 65:17; Rev 21:1). Aspects of heaven already exist on earth. As people are made in God's image, so creation is made in heaven's image. Yet like humans, the earth also exists in an already-not-yet paradox, due to become what in some ways it already is. Humans are not rescued out of the world; the entire created order participates in the redemption of humanity. Christians hold that the created and cursed is the very stuff that gets redeemed and glorified. Though all things die and return to dust, it is out of that same dust that resurrection happens.

Paul put it like this: "Creation was subjected to frustration, not by its own choice, but by the will of the one who subjected it, in hope that the creation itself will be liberated from its bondage to decay and brought into the glorious freedom of the children of God" (Rom 8:20-21 NIV). There's been no shortage of opinion over precisely what Paul had in mind. From the standpoint of evolution, it may be that the frustration to which creation was subjected was the very frustration of death and time (its bondage to entropic decay) that were incapable of accomplishing the redemption God had planned from the beginning. This earth was not meant to be paradise. Creation was not only subjected to death and decay but also to human dominion (talk about frustration!). Yet the creation subjected to humanity's (sinful) dominion is now redeemed by Christ's salvation. God, who created by his word, now re-creates by his word made flesh (John 1:14). New creation remains subjected to humans, but now the humans are not in the ilk of sinful Adam but in the glory of Jesus (Eph 1:10).

When Do We See God?

"OK, one last question. In moving from here to there, what's the time-line? If there's no immaterial soul, do I just lie in the ground until the resurrection? And then if that takes too long, what resurrects? If to be absent from the body is to be present with the Lord (2 Cor 5:8), where exactly am I after I die?" I told you that Dave was a worrier.

It should be said that Christian theology has never thought of heaven in terms of a literal or specific locale, despite the language of location. Given what science reveals, it may make more sense theologically and scientifically to speak of our existence after death not as somewhere else but "some *when* else."[27]

In the ticktock of "flowing time" (earth time), my body—my self—inasmuch as it is made of the stuff of earth, returns to dust in order to participate in the ongoing life of the earth (burial vaults that venerate corpses notwithstanding). I rot in the ground. However, in the context of the "block universe" (heaven time), inasmuch as my life in God is already occurring, my new self immediately enjoys its life in God. It's just as if the time between now and the end of time had already transpired, since in the eternal presence of the block universe it already has. Though we who mourn the dead must abide their absence, the dead themselves experience no passage of time. Re-embodiment is an immediate event outside time.[28] The day of resurrection has already happened on God's clock; we participate in it as we die until that day when the future and present converge and our prayer is answered: God's will is finally done on earth as it is in heaven.[29]

"I think I'll have another piece of pie." Maybe Aunt Bernice was coming around.

Evolution has a forward-facing orientation, propelled by the bang of energy that blasts it into motion from the beginning. However, theology that pairs with evolution works better, not by likewise looking for its energy from the past but by fulfilling its promises with energy from a definite future. While we think of movement through time as heading toward the future, the flow of time runs from the future to the past. Scientifically and theologically, the future is headed toward us. People forecast, but God *backcasts*, breaking backwards from a certain future, pulling experience into ultimate reality.[30] The evil experienced does not mar perfection but rather is being swallowed up in the victory that God has already won since the foundation of the world (1 Cor 15:54; Rev 13:8). This is why hope in God cannot disappoint (Rom 5:5).

"It's like watching the Boston Red Sox win the World Series on DVD after eighty-six years of futility. I review those games for the sheer joy of it. And no matter how anxious I get watching those games over and over, especially with the Sox down three to none to the Yankees for the pennant, the outcome is never in doubt. I'll sweat the DVD but never worry (a big deal for me). The Red Sox win every time." I began to think Dave was coming around too.

In the end it is my relationship to God through Christ, sustained and applied by the Holy Spirit, that is the real guarantor of my continuity from this life into the next. The Trinity, which created as an outpouring of its self-giving generosity, draws all creation back into themself as an ingathering of its generosity. The movement is one of relationship, freedom that leads to embrace due to the ever-giving and ever-beckoning power of sacrificial love. God's love gives and gives up for the sake of creation *and* redemption. Its goal is a new creation that constitutes the final embrace, one wherein no one has been coerced or forced but all enter with joy.

True for the creature, true for creation. We get embraced and so does the earth. Because creatures and creation exist in interrelated solidarity, our new birth signals its new birth. There is a fundamental solidarity between creatures made in God's image and creation in which God's image dwells, a fundamental continuity between creation and new creation. I look forward to perpetual sun-drenched springtime, only one illuminated by the glory of God. How this works out cosmologically is anyone's guess. But instead of the eventual decimation of a universe spun out of control, the earth fried up a billion years hence by an expanding, engorging sun, theology envisions a bigger and better bang, a glorious restoration of heaven and earth set off by Christ's return The ineffable light of God's glory breaks back into the present beckoning us forward toward courageously becoming the people in Christ we already are. And in that day, when we are who we are, we will join with the ancient-future chorus of creation that finally fulfills its purpose in the unending praise of God.

Epilogue

The Real World

I serve on a community bioethics committee for a local hospital where we recently wrestled with the issue of pediatric organ donation after cardiac death. When is it OK to remove organs for consented transplant from a child whose heart has stopped beating irreversibly? The current hospital practice is to wait five minutes after cardiac death. Interestingly, the reason that this hospital goes with five minutes is to provide the deceased with something they term "spiritual wiggle room." (Three other reasons for waiting five minutes include certainty that there is no residual experience of pain, staff comfort levels, and an amount of ambiguity that surrounds a phenomenon called autoresuscitation.) Wanting to be sensitive to various religious views, the hospital reasoned that if there is such a thing as a disembodied soul (which science cannot ascertain), the extra three minutes should provide sufficient time for a soul to depart its body without any threat of desecration on religious grounds.

While there are many sticky issues concerning the practice of pediatric organ donation (the ethics of organ procurement itself among them), this particular conflict between soul survival and organ viability was new to me. As you'd expect, the ethics committee devoted a good deal of time to discussing it. Nonreligious members of the committee were naturally nonplussed. With hundreds of people desperately awaiting organ donation, why risk organ viability by taking extra time for something that, scientifically speaking, we're not even sure occurs? Is this a hospital or a church? I appreciated that the hospital showed such respect for religious belief, but I was troubled that the practice jeopardized potential organ recipients for reasons that might be theologically, as well as scientifically, unfounded.

The ethics committee turned to me (the minister) and to a rabbi for advice. They asked, "How long does it take for a soul to leave a body?" How do I know? My thoughts returned to that science conference so many chapters ago and to the question of whether a clone would have a soul. Evolution, supported by biology, genetics, and neuroscience, implies that whatever it is we mean by *soul*, it's not an entity disconnected from the body. The soul, like the mind, is a function of the brain, made of the same stuff as the rest of the body. Theology concurs: created in God's image, we are whole persons, body and soul, material and spiritual. This time, rather than with fear and uncertainty, I felt I could reply to my colleagues in a way that was more scientifically accurate and biblically faithful. I suggested that "spiritual wiggle room" need not be mandated on theological grounds. If the *body* is dead after two minutes, there is no detached *living soul* that survives it. Bodies are not containers for persons but are the persons themselves. To believe in the resurrection of the dead is to believe in the resurrection of dead bodies, just like Jesus himself, a whole flesh and bone person and not a ghost (Luke 24:39) or any other sort of immaterial apparition. The ethics committee agreed that a lower time threshold for pediatric organ donation could be ethical (given that the other concerns were likewise addressed).

Not long after, I received a call from the hospital where a newborn from our congregation was fighting for his life. I arrived at the NICU amid utter distress. The baby was hooked up to every sort of tube and machine. The incubating lights blared against his translucent skin. His little heart beat rapidly. The heroic nurses and doctors in the NICU were doing everything they could. But the prognosis was grim. This baby was not going to make it. And he didn't. As we sadly gathered to bury their child, the parents needed to hear that their baby was safe with Jesus now. As the minister presiding over the child's funeral, what do I say to the parents? What do I preach at the graveside? The body of their baby still lay in the small coffin before us; could I safely (and truthfully) say he was anywhere but *there* right now? It is in such tragic moments that our faith matters most. But if faith is going to matter, it must correspond with the *way things are* rather than with the way we want things to be.

Does the fact that we are whole persons mean that after we die it is all ashes to ashes and dust to dust with no hope for ourselves in the meantime? What did Paul mean when he said that to be "away from the body" is to be "at home with the Lord" (2 Cor 5:8) if he did not mean immediately? What sort of comfort does faith give a family if it tells them that their baby decomposes in the ground until Jesus returns and puts us all back together again? The temptation here is to separate theology and science and give ourselves our own "spiritual wiggle room" so as to assuage our grief. But wiggle room is unnecessary here too. By integrating theology and science, an answer emerges that is both spiritually assuring and scientifically plausible. Physics suggest that in the ticktock of earthly time as we experience it, the child's body indeed returns to the earth to participate in biology's ongoing life. However, in heaven time (the physics of a "block universe"; see page 120), the child and her redeemed new creation enjoys immediate life in God. The Bible describes believers as dead and gone to heaven already even as we walk around on earth (Col 3:3). At the same time, on a future day, "the trumpet will sound, the dead will be raised imperishable, and we will be changed" (1 Cor 15:52 NIV). So whether dead or alive, in Christ we are always with God.

Just as "flowing time" and "block universe" conceptions of time exist simultaneously in physics, so earth time and heaven time simultaneously exist. The temporal distance between these two conceptions of time will collapse at the end of time. But even as that collapse is destined to occur in the future, in God's time it has happened already. So has the day of resurrection, which is how Paul can write that we are seated with Christ now (Eph 2:6), and how I could preach that the little baby boy is safely in the arms of Jesus even as he lies buried in the ground. The day of resurrection has already happened on God's clock even though we still wait for it on our own clock. OK, so I didn't preach all of *that* at the graveside, but the hope of the resurrection I did preach was preached with a confidence upheld by all of God's truth, the scientific and the theological.

If you've made it through this book, then you probably still have questions. Science and faith can feel like a hard fit, especially when it comes to evolution. But one reason I think integrating faith and evolution makes us wary is because of the ways that religion's opponents have employed evolution in their own arsenal of arguments against faith. They make the illogical assumption that to naturally explain a phenomenon is to prove that God is not involved in it. I've tried to make the exact opposite assertion. We instinctively thank God when the weather breaks or the illness heals or the baby is born—all natural occurrences.

Just because you can describe the diversification of biological life without specific mention of Genesis doesn't mean that God is not the Creator. The fact is, when you look at the marvel of evolution and its creativity, it's harder to imagine God not being the Creator. Nature is God's handiwork. Natural explanations describe how God works and illustrate his creativity.

Nevertheless, for many, allowing evolution into one's theology remains a scary proposition. Acknowledging that the earth is older than the Bible appears to say or that people emerged out of millions of years of evolution rather than in a moment are costly concessions to make. Add to that evolution's implication that God is a God for whom death is part of the plan, and quickly the theological price tag becomes too expensive to pay. It's simply easier to deny evolution. You can say that God instilled creation with apparent age and that science is just deluded and a waste of time. You can say that—but you don't need to say that. If evolution is a correct description of how life emerged and developed on earth, denying it doesn't make it false, any more than denying God renders him nonexistent. Moreover, if the evidence for evolution is accurate, as science attests, and nature bears witness to the handiwork of God, then rejecting evolution becomes, in effect, a rejection of God. This is my worry. More than worrying that evolution jeopardizes Christian faith, I worry that rejecting evolution truncates Christian faith. Again, for faith to matter, it needs to correspond to the way things actually are, rather than how we want things to be.

This may sound like a compromised theology. But it's not. It is an adjusted theology, but that's nothing new. Throughout church history, Christians have had their understanding and interpretation of Scripture shaped by discovery and experience. This doesn't make the Bible any less true. If anything, the more we learn about the world, the closer our theological approximations come to the truth itself. God is an infinite and independent reality. Even when we know everything we can know about him, there will still be infinitely more to know. This is what makes theology so interesting. Every time we think we have God figured out, some experience or new realization comes along that unmasks our convictions as idols in need of breaking. It's what makes science so interesting too. The natural world resists our expectations that it function as we predict, forcing us to adjust our expectations and expand our boundaries of comprehension. To repeat a sentence: both God and his world as science unveils it constantly blow our minds.

I think this a good thing. You can sit through freshman biology, hear the professor explain life's origins and development through genetic variation and natural selection, and then watch your faith crumble as God is moved to the periphery. Or you can sit in that same class and praise God for his ingenuity and creativity—even when that creativity runs counter to your expectations. For an analogous example from theology, take the incarnation. Already Christians stretch the boundaries of faith by assenting to God's revelation of himself in the flesh and blood person of Jesus Christ. God's creativity runs counter to your expectations here too. Even if you believed that Almighty God would stoop to reveal himself in a finite human being, who'd ever believe he'd choose to reveal himself as a homeless-poor-crucified-as-a-criminal kind of human being? If you can believe that, believing that God likewise reveals something of himself in the variation and natural selection of evolution is hardly a stretch. Still, to stretch faith is a far cry from destroying faith. If anything, a stretched faith takes in a little bit more of the infinite realities of God. To be a serious Christian is not only to seek truth but to find truth as revealed by God, both in Scripture *and* in nature.

Evolution is a natural account of life on earth, not a godless account. Much of what we already hold to be true about God—his relational nature, his mind-blowing creativity and generosity, his self-giving love—all of these characteristics can be observed in the evolutionary epic. Evolution demonstrates that all organic life is related. Everything comes from the same stuff, just as the Bible teaches, made by the same hand. The variety of life and its extravagant complexity, most of which remains undiscovered, elicits wonder and awe by even the most atheistic. That life has emerged as it has demonstrated immense ingenuity on the part of nature, a capability that's easy for the faithful to attribute to God's generous endowment. That so much death and sacrifice has occurred over the course of earth's history in order to bring about human life only mirrors the sacrificial character of God and barely approximates the ultimate sacrifice of himself in Christ for the sins of the world. By allowing evolution within a Christian framework, we get to praise God for the way he actually operates. Science no longer functions as a contrary, atheisti enterprise, even if some scientists themselves choose to reject God.

For many skeptics of Christianity, evolution ranks right after "th problem of evil" as a reason for disbelief. Who needs God when evolu tion by itself accounts for everything? But evolution itself has no stake i whether or not God exists, despite some scientists' insistence on inter preting evolution this way. Ironically, some Christians defend their posi tion by attacking data about nature found in nature rather than scientists interpretations of the data. We forget that scientific data and scientists *interpretations* of scientific data are not the same thing. Reading natur through a Christian grid can affirm the creativity and character of Go without denying evolution's premises. God is the God of both evolutio and the Bible. Such a read effectively removes evolution as an obstacle t faith. Moreover, allowing for evolution within a Christian framework no only removes this obstacle, but it addresses the first obstacle too. I'm no saying that Darwinism solves the "problem of evil," but evolution doe place *some* of what we understand as "evil" within the rubric of a cross shaped creation. It accounts for the death and disease that necessitate biological growth. It accounts for the death that results from a free process creation (see page 105). Life gives its life for the sake of new life God's own sacrificial and loving nature imprints itself on a world that i not yet what he intends it to be. The cruciform of Christian salvatio turns out to be the shape of creation too.

Given the shape of creation, many theologians (and preachers!) no regard the "new heaven and the new earth" of Revelation as a more plau sible basis from which to expound on God's purposes for creation tha the "in the beginning" of Genesis. Granted, the book of Revelation ha its own interpretive challenges, yet its central thrust remains clear. In th scope of redemptive history, the trajectory of creation is aimed finall toward new creation (Rev 21:1-5), the reconciliation of all things i Christ (Col 1:19-20). Inasmuch as Scripture moves toward a certai future that already exists in God, creation's *destiny* may deserve mor emphasis as creation's starting point.

Rather than just a response to human sin, redemption can be viewe as part of the plan from the start. And because God always finishes wha he starts, the Scripture can speak of new creation as having alread happened. "I *saw* a new heaven and a new earth," John writes in Revelation 21:1 (NIV, italics mine), "the first heaven and the first earth had passed away." The "Lamb of God, who takes away the sin of the world" (John 1:29 NIV) appears in Revelation as "the Lamb that was slain from the creation of the world" (Rev 13:8 NIV). Evolutionary death for the sake of new life foreshadows Christ's redemptive work—a redemption that was always in the works, for both the creature and the creation (Rom 8:20).

In Christ we are new creations *now*, Paul writes, "the old has gone, the new has come" (2 Cor 5:17 NIV). Granted, being a new creation doesn't mean we always act like one. Our experience has not yet caught up to reality. We've yet to become who we already are in Christ. In Romans 7, Paul famously depicts this dilemma as a war waging inside his soul. On the one hand, "I love God's law with all my heart," he wrote (7:22 NLT). To love my neighbor, to forgive those who wrong me, to care for the poor, and to speak the truth, these are all good and right and the ways I want to live my life. Yet on the other hand, I do not love, I do not forgive, I don't care about the poor, and I lie without cause. "I do not understand my own actions," he groaned. "For I do not do what I want, but I do the very thing I hate" (7:15). A war wages within, Paul writes, but we are not its only casualties. In Romans 8 Paul cites the polluting, toxic waste human sin has spewed onto the entire landscape, both physically and metaphysically, causing frustration, futility, and bondage for the earth too. Evolution shows how all living things are interrelated—we all come from the same dirt. And thus what's true for the creature is true for creation. We groan and the creation groans too. Together, we're all out of sorts.

While the *will to survive* that is inherent to the evolutionary epic predates human sinfulness, reading aspects of that *will to survive* as a *survival of the fittest* may reflect sin's effect on evolution itself. Clearly humanity's negative impact on the environment has severely disrupted ecosystems. Species have become extinct solely due to human causes. Yet just as creation groans alongside creatures made in God's image, so shall our redemption be shared by the earth. The dust of creation to which all living things return when they die is the same dust out of which resurrection and new creation emerges. Ours is not a throwaway planet any more than our bodies are mere jars of clay to be carelessly tossed aside. We believe in the resurrection *of the body* and all things made new. As new creations already, we can anticipate our future redemption in the present—in those moments when we do love our neighbors, when we do forgive those who wrong us, and when we do care for the poor and speak the truth; these are foretastes of glory divine. Likewise, we can point to our future redemption alongside creation—by the kind of cars that we choose to drive (or not), the trash we recycle, the light bulbs and the hot water we use, the money we spend and give, and the restraints which we impose upon our consumption and waste.

As science plows forward, evolution's assertions themselves undergo revision. New discoveries shed light on the way genes function, how climates change, how the universe itself operates. Each of these discoveries, once confirmed, will possibly shed new light on how we understand God. For some, this is disturbing. It feels as if the foundation on which faith is built is more rocky than rock solid (Matt 7:24). This shaky feeling leads to an indifferent or compartmentalized approach to science: "Why care about evolution? My faith defines my reality. The Lord works in mysterious ways—beyond the reach of science. Just because science can explain phenomena doesn't make it so." Science is bound by its temporal limitations; it has nothing to say about eternal reality. Evolution cannot prove God doesn't exist. "Survival of the fittest" hardly accounts for love or beauty or community or other aspects of life people experience daily.

And yet, while Christianity's claims are grounded in supernatural events that science cannot explain (most importantly the resurrection of Jesus), its claims are also grounded in ordinary occurrences within history and the natural world. The remarkable growth of the church, the beauty of creation, and the makeup of human nature are all understood by Christians to be manifestations of God (Rom 1:20). Yet each is also subject to scientific study and interpretation. This is what makes Christianity so compelling. Christians have always believed all truth to be God's truth, implying that faith and science, despite differences when it comes to explaining *why*, nevertheless should agree in regard to *what is*. Science informs the way we interact with our world, it inextricably aids in fighting disease, understanding organisms and growth, safeguarding the environment, and planning for the future. Science matters whether we care about it or not. And because science matters, it warrants theological reflection.

Christianity must remain faithful to the biblical narrative as its source for theological reflection, but at the same time, Christianity should herald scientific discovery as an accurate description of the universe on which theology reflects. As reliable witnesses of nature, we can only become more reliable witnesses to God.

Notes

Introduction

1. John Caputo, *Philosophy and Theology* (Nashville: Abingdon, 2006) 17.
2. Ibid., 18.

1. Hello, God?

1. For the program guide to the MIT-Harvard Conference on Genetic Technology and Society, March 13-14, 1999, see http://b435-boas.stanford.edu/home/other_projects/gene_conf/program_one_side.pdf.
2. John Polkinghorne, *Exploring Reality: The Intertwining of Science and Religion* (New Haven, Conn.: Yale University Press, 2005), 128.
3. Daniel C. Dennett, *Breaking the Spell: Religion as Natural Phenomenon* (New York: Viking, 2006), 220.
4. Called "apophatic theology" (or the "negative way"), it attempts to describe God by negation, that is, to speak of God only in terms of what may *not* be said about God. You will find this expressed most commonly in Eastern Christian traditions, such as the writings of Gregory of Nyssa or Basil the Great. For a contemporary description, see Vladimir Lossky, *The Mystical Tradition of the Eastern Church* (Crestwood, N.Y.: St. Vladimir's Seminary Press, 1976), 23–43.
5. Daniel Harrell, "A Day at the Genetic Circus," *Regeneration Quarterly* 5, no. 3 (Fall, 1999): 10.
6. Dolly was the first mammal to be cloned successfully from an adult somatic cell. She was cloned at the Roslin Institute in Scotland. Her birth was announced in February 1997. She lived six years.
7. Gilbert Meilander, "Begetting and Cloning," *First Things* 74 (June/July 1997): 41–43.
8. One reaction to this assertion is that the comatose or the mentally disabled or the very young or the very old will suffer further marginalization if they end up bereft of their status as embodied souls. With limited cognitive ability, would their "souls" be limited too? Not necessarily. The soul is not determined by the brain, just hard-wired to it. The fact is that the brain itself undergoes physiological changes in response to learning and experience, including religious experience.
9. Though as Tufts University religion professor Dr. Heather Curtis reminds me, evolution and Christianity have not always been in conflict. The metaphor of warfare obscures a long history of conversation and creative interaction (see David N. Livingstone, *Darwin's Forgotten Defenders: The Encounter between Evangelical Theology and Evolutionary Thought* [Grand Rapids, Mich.: Eerdmans, 1987]). In fact, Christians have always been interested in learning from science and reconciling it with faith. What I am doing here is not new.
10. Edward O. Wilson, *Consilience: The Unity of Knowledge* (New York: Knopf, 1999), 265.

11. Dennett, *Breaking the Spell*, 107.

12. Mark Noll, *The Scandal of the Evangelical Mind* (Grand Rapids, Mich.: Eerdmans), 199.

13. Frank Ryan, *Darwin's Blind Spot: Evolution Beyond Natural Selection* (Boston: Houghton Mifflin, 2002), 7.

14. Dennett, *Breaking the Spell*, 60.

15. Ryan, *Darwin's Blind Spot*, 13.

16. Kenneth R. Miller, *Finding Darwin's God: A Scientist's Search for Common Ground between God and Evolution* (New York: Harper Perennial, 1999), 21.

17. Ibid., 80.

2. I'll Be a Monkey's Cousin

1. "I was always interested in anatomy and how things work. . . . But I stay away from human evolution. . . . It's not a field for gentlemen. Those anthropologists are savage." Farish A. Jenkins Jr., Professor of Paleontology, Harvard University, as interviewed by Andrew Rimas, "He Landed the Fish That Landed Itself," *Boston Globe*, May 22, 2006.

2. Rimas, "He Landed the Fish."

3. Keith B. Miller, "An Evolving Creation: Oxymoron or Fruitful Insight?" in *Perspectives on an Evolving Creation*, ed. Keith B. Miller (Grand Rapids, Mich.: Eerdmans, 2003), 7.

4. "No serious biologist today doubts the theory of evolution to explain the marvelous complexity and diversity of life. In fact, the relatedness of all species through the mechanism of evolution is such a profound foundation for the understanding of all biology that it is difficult to imagine how one would study life without it." Francis S. Collins, *The Language of God: A Scientist Presents Evidence for Belief* (New York: Free, 2006), 99.

5. Loren Haarsma, "Does Science Exclude God? Natural Law, Chance, Miracles and Scientific Practice" in *Perspectives on an Evolving Creation*, ed. Keith B. Miller (Grand Rapids, Mich.: Eerdmans, 2003), 93.

6. Miller, "An Evolving Creation," 11.

7. Naturally occurring mutations in DNA arise at a rate of about one error every one hundred million base pairs per generation. (That means that since we all have two genomes of three billion base pairs each—one from each parent—we all have roughly sixty new mutations that were not present in either of our parents.) Most of these mutations occur in parts of the genome that are not essential, and therefore they have little or no consequence. The ones that fall in the more vulnerable parts of the genome are generally harmful and are thus rapidly culled out of the population because they reduce reproductive fitness. On rare occasions, by chance a mutation will arise that offers a slight degree of selective advantage and will have a slightly higher likelihood of being passed on to future offspring. Collins, *The Language of God*, 131.

8. My thanks for the specifics to Dr. Cindy Lu, Harvard Medical School.

9. Ernst Mayr, *What Evolution Is* (New York: Basic, 2001), 120.

10. Ibid.

11. Martinez J. Hewlett, "Biological Evolution in Science and Theology" in *Bridging Science and Religion*, ed. Ted Peters and Gaymon Bennett (Minneapolis: Fortress, 2003), 70.

12. Mayr, *What Evolution Is*, 284.

13. Ibid., 212.

14. Ian G. Barbour, *Religion and Science: Historical and Contemporary Issues* (New York: HarperSanFrancisco, 1997), 222.

15. Ryan, *Darwin's Blind Spot*, 16–17.

16. Mayr, *What Evolution Is*, 190.

17. "One important thing to know is that there are core, conserved pathways and processes that do not differ greatly between the simplest and most complex organism. Embellishments to these core processes form much of the variability we see. In that sense, the process is steady and continuous." Comments by Dr. Cindy Lu, June 18, 2007.

18. Mark W. Kirschner and John C. Gerhart, *The Plausibility of Life* (New Haven, Conn.: Yale University Press, 2005), 224.

19. Stuart Kauffman, "Prolegomenon to a General Biology," in *Debating Design: From Darwin to DNA*, ed. William A. Dembski and Michael Ruse (Cambridge: Cambridge University Press, 2006), 167.

20. Mayr, *What Evolution Is*, 105.

21. Francisco J. Ayala, "Design without Designer: Darwin's Greatest Discovery," in *Debating Design: From Darwin to DNA*, 64.

22. Ibid.

23. "A few fossil lineages are remarkably complete. This is true, for instance, for the lineage that leads from the therapsid reptiles to the mammals." Mayr, *What Evolution Is*, 14.

24. Miller, "An Evolving Creation," 153.

25. Miller, *Finding Darwin's God*, 40.

26. Miller, "An Evolving Creation," 161.

27. "The overwhelming evidence of anatomy, fossils and molecular biology suggest that the chimpanzees are our nearest relatives and that they are more closely related to people than they are to gorillas." Mayr, *What Evolution Is*, 237.

28. David L. Wilcox, "Finding Adam: The Genetics of Human Origins," in *Perspectives on an Evolving Creation*, ed. Keith B. Miller (Grand Rapids, Mich.: Eerdmans, 2003), 235–36.

29. More precisely, the human genome and the genomes of the two chimpanzee species group together as a *monophyletic clade*. The term implies 1) that the organisms in question all have a common ancestor, and 2) that all the descendants of that ancestor are included. Ibid., 238.

30. Miller, *Finding Darwin's God*, 59.

31. DNA (deoxyribonucleic acid) carries your genetic information in each of your cells. RNA (ribonucleic acid) plays several important roles. It is most well known as an intermediate molecule during the translation of a DNA sequence into a protein product. However, it can also play an active role in the activation or repression of gene activity.

32. Kirschner and Gerhart, *The Plausibility of Life*, 221; Collins, *The Language of God*, 102–4.

33. Mayr, *What Evolution Is*, 93.

34. A recent comparison of samples of human mitochondrial DNA suggests that humans have descended from a woman who lived in Africa 140,000 to 290,000 years ago. There were likely many other women alive at the time of the so-called "mitochondrial Eve," but their lines of maternal inheritance have died out.

35. My thanks to Harvard developmental biologist Joshua Mugford for this insight.

36. Even though the lineages of humans and chimpanzees separated at least six million years ago, the highly complex hemoglobin molecules of these two species are still virtually identical. Mayr, *What Evolution Is*, 36.

37. "Human embryos, for example, form a yolk sac during the early stages of development. In birds and reptiles, the very same sac surrounds a nutrient-rich yolk, from which it draws nourishment to support the growth of the embryo. Human egg cells have no comparable stores of yolk. Being placental mammals, we draw nourishment from the bodies of our mothers, but we form a yolk sac anyway, a completely empty one. That curiously empty yolk sac is just one sign that the ancestry of mammals could be found in egg-laying reptile-like animals, a notion that is confirmed in the fossil record." Miller, *Finding Darwin's God*, 100–1.

Having said this, it is important to note that the mammalian yolk sac is not useless. Embryonic cells interact with cells outside the embryo (such as those in the yolk sac) to do things such as setting up the basic body plan, determining head from tail, for instance. From comments by Dr. Cindy Lu, June 18, 2007.

38. Dan Petersen, "What's the Big Deal about Intelligent Design?" *American Spectator*, December 22, 2005, http://spectator.org/.

39. Wilcox, "Finding Adam," 239.

40. Ibid., 240.

41. Howard J. Van Till, "Is the Universe Capable of Evolving?" in *Perspectives on an Evolving Creation*, ed. Keith B. Miller (Grand Rapids, Mich.: Eerdmans, 2003), 319.

42. Barbour, *Religion and Science*, 215.

43. George L. Murphy, "Christology, Evolution and the Cross," in *Perspectives on an Evolving Creation*, 384.

44. Deborah B. Haarsma and Jennifer Wiseman, "An Evolving Cosmos," in *Perspectives on an Evolving Creation*, 106.

45. Early in this century, astronomers noticed that distant galaxies had peculiar light spectra. Specifically, the galaxies' light spectra were shifted toward the red end of the spectrum. In 1929, astronomer Edwin Hubble compared the galaxies' spectra with their distances, which he calculated using various methods. He showed that the amount of "red shift" was proportional to distance. Hubble and others realized that the most obvious explanation for the "red shift" was that the galaxies were receding from Earth and each other, and the farther the galaxy, the faster the recession.

46. Barbour, *Religion and Science*, 179.

47. Hans Beta worked this for all elements. He was able to show how the elements (hydrogen and helium were around from the Big Bang) were created in the first generation stars and also able to calculate what the abundances for each element should be. This agrees with what we measure. Comment by physicist Dr. John U. Free, Eastern Nazarene College, and Harvard University, July 5, 2007.

48. Miller, *Finding Darwin's God*, 79.

49. Dr. Gordon Hugenberger asks the same question about the turning water to wine at Cana (John 2:9). Was that a deception too? The answer as it pertains to creation is whether we should view creation as a miraculous event, outside God's "ordinary" ways of doing things. I'd suggest that creation falls under God's ordinary providence, while turning water to wine was a miracle.

50. Stephen W. Hawking, *A Brief History of Time* (New York: Bantam, 1996), 23.

51. Ibid., 34.

52. Collins, *The Language of God*, 89.

53. Miller, *Finding Darwin's God*, 69.

54. Barbour, *Religion and Science*, 214.

55. "The most obscure origination of a core process is the creation of the first prokaryotic cell [a unicellular microorganism that lacks a distinct nucleus and membrane-bound organelles]. The novelty and complexity of the cell is so far beyond anything inanimate in the world today that we are left baffled by how it was achieved . . . Perhaps, for all we know, life originated only once." Kirschner and Gerhart, *The Plausibility of Life*, 256.

56. Particle Data Group, "What Holds It Together? Strong," http://particleadventure.org/frameless/strong.html (accessed June 20, 2007).

57. Miller, *Finding Darwin's God*, 228.

58. As quoted in Collins, *The Language of God*, 74.

59. George Johnson, "Oh for the Simple Days of the Big Bang,' *New York Times*, October 8, 2006.

60. "Perhaps . . . all of these constants are forced to have these values because there is no alternative. Perhaps the great holy grail of physics, that 'theory of everything,' will show why they must be this way, just as surely as two plus two must equal 4, and thus show that God had no choice." Owen Gingerich, *God's Universe* (Cambridge, Mass.: The Belknap Press of Harvard University Press, 2006), 58.

61. "One of the major endeavors in physics today is the search for a new theory that will incorporate them both—a quantum theory of gravity." Hawking, *A Brief History of Time*, 12.

62. Jim Holt, "Unstrung,' *New Yorker* n.v. (October 2, 2006): 88, http://www.newyorker.com/archive/2006/10/02/061002crat_atlarge (accessed June 20, 2007).

63. Hawking, *A Brief History of Time*, 58.

64. A unified theory that pulls together gravity (relativity) and quantum mechanics remains the ultimate goal of physics. The current vogue theory is called "string theory," which mathematically hypothesizes even smaller entities called *strings* that strum throughout the universe. See Brian Greene, *The Elegant Universe: Superstrings, Hidden Dimensions and the Quest for the Ultimate Theory* (New York: Norton, 2003).

65. Hawking, *A Brief History of Time*, 57.

66. Miller, *Finding Darwin's God*, 201.

67. Ibid., 207.

68. Barbour, *Religion and Science*, 173.

69. Paul Bloom, "Is God an Accident?" *Atlantic Monthly* 296 (December 2005).

3. What Happens When I Think Too Much

1. Gabriel Fackre, *The Christian Story*, 3rd ed. (Grand Rapids, Mich.: Eerdmans, 1996), 65.

2. Stanley J. Grenz, *Theology for the Community of God* (Nashville: Broadman & Holman, 1994), 147.

3. John Jefferson Davis, "Response to Howard J. Van Till," in *Three Views of Creation and Evolution*, ed. J. P. Moreland and John Mark Reynolds (Grand Rapids, Mich.: Zondervan, 1999), 227.

4. Fackre, *The Christian Story*, 63.

5. Ibid., 65.

6. John H. Sailhamer, "Genesis" in *The Expositor's Bible Commentary*, ed. Frank E. Gaebelein (Grand Rapids, Mich.: Zondervan, 1990), 38.

7. I take for granted that in heaven no one would ever reject love since accepting God's love is what got you there.

8. This line of logic is known in theological circles as the "freewill defense." It's been used for centuries to counter the problem of evil that occurs in the presence of a God who is loving and good. It states that while evil is awful, it is necessary in order for humans to be more than just hand puppets. I'll return to it later.

9. Fackre, *The Christian Story*, 68.

10. Sarah Coakley, "A New Way of Looking at God and Evolution," *Harvard Divinity Bulletin* 35 (Spring/Summer 2007): 11.

11. Hugh Ross and Gleason L. Archer, "The Day-Age View," in *The Genesis Debate: Three Views on the Days of Creation*, ed. David G. Hagopian (Mission Viejo, Calif.: Crux, 2001), 123.

12. Ibid., 210.

13. John F. Haught, *God after Darwin: A Theology of Evolution* (Boulder, Colo.: Westview, 2000), 14.

14. Hawking, *A Brief History of Time*, 11.

15. Arthur R. Peacocke, *Evolution: The Disguised Friend of Faith?* (Philadelphia: Templeton, 2004), 139.

16. John F. Haught, "Darwin, Design and Divine Providence," in *Debating Design: From Darwin to DNA*, ed. William A. Dembski and Michael Ruse (Cambridge: Cambridge University Press, 2006), 232–33.

17. Haught, *God after Darwin*, 22.

18. Peacocke, *Evolution*, 9.

19. Though as my friend Joel Roth-Nater observes, the same could be said of God's redemptive work throughout history. Look at all the twists and turns in Israelite history, all the things that had to line up for Christ to appear. God could have just accomplished what he wanted by divine *fiat*, but that does not appear to be his *modus operandi*.

20. The Cambrian explosion was an interval of about 70 million years, from 570 million to 500 million years ago. The period was a time of steadily increasing oxygen content in the atmosphere and oceans, making life that could derive energy from respiration possible. All major bilaterian (two-sided) phyla with conspicuously fossilizable hard parts make their appearance here. Stephen Jay Gould, *The Structure of Evolutionary Theory* (Cambridge, Mass.: Harvard University Press, 2002), 1155.

Many biologists doubt that the Cambrian explosion ever really occurred. Some think it is an artifact. What really happened, they believe, is that about 550 million years ago a change resulted in a much greater likelihood of fossilization. They reason that the "sudden" appearance of multicellular animals in the fossil record does not so much reflect a dramatic change in what animals were living as it reflects the preservability of those animals that did exist. They were simply more likely to make an appearance in the fossil record. Darrel R. Falk, *Coming to Peace with Science: Bridging the World between Faith and Biology* (Downers Grove, Ill.: InterVarsity, 2004), 94.

21. Collins, *The Language of God*, 148–49.

22. Ibid., 227.

23. String theory at this point is more of a hunch than a theory. Holt, "Unstrung," 86–91.

24. Charles Darwin, *The Origin of Species* (1859; repr., Chicago: Encyclopedia Britannica, 1952), 32.

25. Ayala, "Design without Designer," 56.

26. As Reinhold Niebuhr was known to say on many occasions. See http://www.religion-online.org/showarticle.asp?title=989.

27. "Neolithic" relates to the cultural period beginning around 10,000 B.C. in the Middle East and later elsewhere and is characterized by the development of agriculture and the making of polished stone implements. James P. Hurd, "Hominids in the Garden?" in *Perspectives on an Evolving Creation*, ed. Keith B. Miller (Grand Rapids, Mich.: Eerdmans, 2003), 224.

28. Ibid.

29. *Hominid* is the name for a primate of the family *Hominidae*, of which *Homo sapiens* is the only extant species. There are no cave dwellers currently walking the planet.

30. Wilcox, "Finding Adam," 252–53.

31. That is, *made* instead of *begotten*, which then contradicts my theological logic in regard to cloning—see ch. 1, p. 6. Borrowing language from the Nicene Creed, I suggested how, *theologically speaking*, children *begotten* as a gift of marital love are somehow distinguishable from children *made* as cloned products of personal preference. Not that my logic was particularly logical—at least not genetically speaking.

32. Miller, *Finding Darwin's God*, 181.

4. E-Harmony

1. John Polkinghorne, *Belief in God in an Age of Science* (New Haven, Conn.: Yale University Press, 1998), 44.

2. Haarsma, "Does Science Exclude God?" 78.

3. Barbara Brown Taylor, *The Luminous Web: Essays on Science and Religion* (Boston: Cowley, 2000), 33.

4. Ibid., 99.

5. The following analogy from nutrition is taken from Michael Pollan, "Unhappy Meals," *New York Times Magazine* n.v. (January 28, 2007): 38–70.

6. Ibid.

7. Polkinghorne, *Exploring Reality*, 31.

8. Nancey Murphy, *Anglo-American Postmodernity: Philosophical Perspectives on Science, Religion and Ethics* (Boulder, Colo.: Westview, 1997), 165.

9. Polkinghorne, *Belief in God*, 47.

10. Haught, *God after Darwin*, 111.

11. Alister E. McGrath, *The Science of God: An Introduction to Scientific Theology* (London: T&T Clark, 2004), 20.

12. Ibid., 107.

13. Steven Pinker, *How the Mind Works* (New York: Norton, 1997), 376.

14. McGrath, *The Science of God*, 143.

15. Polkinghorne, *Exploring Reality*, 5.

16. This is a term associated with Intelligent Design proponents. It asserts that some biological entities are so complex that they cannot be explained by evolution.

17. Murphy, *Anglo-American Postmodernity*, 196.

18. Warren S. Brown, "Reconciling Scientific and Biblical Portraits of Human Nature," in *Whatever Happened to the Soul? Scientific and Theological Portraits of Human Nature*, ed Warren S. Brown, Nancey Murphy, and H. Newton Malony (Minneapolis: Fortress 1998), 215.

19. Polkinghorne, *Belief in God*, 50.

20. Barbour, *Religion and Science*, 219.

21. Polkinghorne, *Exploring Reality*, 109.

22. Taylor, *The Luminous Web*, 90.

5. Believolution

1. Van Till, "Is the Universe Capable of Evolving?" 330.

2. Ibid., 331.

3. Deism is the belief, based solely on reason, in a God who created the universe and then abandoned it, assuming no control over life, no influence on natural phenomena and no supernatural revelation.

4. See p. 42.

5. Collins, *The Language of God*, 53.

6. Howard J. Van Till, "The Fully Gifted Creation: Theistic Evolution," in *Three Views of Creation and Evolution*, ed. J. P. Moreland and John Mark Reynolds (Grand Rapids, Mich.: Zondervan, 1999), 188.

7. John Polkinghorne, "The Inbuilt Potentiality of Creation," in *Debating Design From Darwin to DNA*, ed. William A. Dembski and Michael Ruse (Cambridge Cambridge University Press, 2006), 251.

8. Conrad Hyers, "Comparing Biblical and Scientific Maps of Origins," in *Perspectives on an Evolving Creation*, ed. Keith B. Miller (Grand Rapids, Mich.: Eerdmans, 2003), 32

9. Denis Edwards, *The God of Evolution* (New York: Paulist, 1999), 31.

10. Ibid., 25.

11. Joan Roughgarden, *Evolution and Christian Faith: Reflections of an Evolutionary Biologist* (Washington, D.C.: Island, 2006), 73.

12. Ibid., 77.

13. Ibid., 78.

14. Ibid., 106.

15. Haught, *God after Darwin*, 25.

16. Haught, "Darwin, Design and Divine Providence," 242.

17. Ibid., 243.

18. Van Till, "The Fully Gifted Creation," 168–69.

19. If you're bothered by comparing God to an honest casino owner, remember that Jesus used the analogy of a *dishonest* employee to set an example for the way Christians should behave (Luke 16:8).

20. David Campbell and Keith B. Miller, "The 'Cambrian Explosion': A Challenge to Evolutionary Theory?" in *Perspectives on an Evolving Creation*, ed. Keith B. Miller (Grand Rapids, Mich.: Eerdmans, 2003), 202.

21. See p. 35.

22. Haught, *God after Darwin*, 35.

23. The previously mentioned precise mathematical properties of gravity, electromagnetism, the "strong" nuclear force, the "weak" nuclear force, and the expansion rate of the universe.

24. Polkinghorne, *Belief in God*, 11.

25. Though there are departments that are trying to mix chemistry, physics, math, and biology in the same building so that you might get a collaboration that would address gene diversity modeled with a mathematical equation that takes into account biophysics, biochemistry, and gene function. Notions of theophysics and theochemistry are still being sorted out.

26. Roughgarden, *Evolution and Christian Faith*, 37.

27. Barbour, *Religion and Science*, 238.

28. Haught, *God after Darwin*, 30.

29. Ibid.

30. Ibid., 168.

31. Peacocke, *Evolution*, 134.

32. Haught, *God after Darwin*, 182.

33. Robert John Russell, "Special Providence and Genetic Mutation: A New Defense of Theistic Evolution," in *Perspectives on an Evolving Creation*, 336.

34. Roughgarden, *Evolution and Christian Faith*, 52.

35. Haarsma, "Does Science Exclude God?" 77.

36. Coakley, "A New Way of Looking at God and Evolution," 10.

37. Ibid., 243.

38. This idea was derived from a conversation with Dr. Gordon Hugenberger, February 27, 2007. For a further exposition of Hugenberger's views on the cruciform character of creation, see his sermon "Science, Creation, and the Cross" preached at Park Street Church, Boston, on February 3, 2008, and available at http://www.park-street.org/sermon_audio.

39. Miller, *Finding Darwin's God*, 245.

40. Van Till, "The Fully Gifted Creation," 208.

41. Ross and Archer, "The Day-Age Reply," 210.

42. Lee Irons and Meredith G. Kline, "The Framework Reply," in *The Genesis Debate: Three Views on the Days of Creation*, ed. David G. Hagopian (Mission Viejo, Calif.: Crux, 2001), 285.

43. I should acknowledge, however, that new textual and archaeological evidence can alter current biblical translations just as future scientific discovery can alter current scientific understanding. As we do not possess all the possible information in regard to natural reality, so too we do not possess any of the original documents of holy writ.

44. This entire paragraph follows Gordon J. Wenham, "Genesis," in *The New Bible Commentary: 21st Century Edition*, 4th ed., ed. D. A. Carson et al. (Downers Grove, Ill.: InterVarsity, 1994), 39–40.

45. Hyers, "Comparing Biblical and Scientific Maps," 32.

46. Lee Irons and Meredith G. Kline, "The Framework Response to the Day-Age View" in *The Genesis Debate: Three Views on the Days of Creation*, ed. David G. Hagopian (Mission Viejo, Calif.: Crux, 2001), 184.

47. Lee Irons and Meredith G. Kline, "The Framework View," in *The Genesis Debate. Three Views on the Days of Creation*, ed. David G. Hagopian (Mission Viejo, Calif.: Crux, 2001), 222.

48. Wenham, "Genesis," 59.

49. Irons and Kline, "The Framework View," 245.

50. "Old Testament Hebrew contains relatively few nouns. Multiple meanings were the norm, not the exception. When vocabulary is limited, synonyms are rare." Ross and Archer, "The Day-Age Reply," 200.

51. Wenham, "Genesis," 60.

52. Ibid., 88.

53. You might go as far as to suggest that Adam's sleep and giving up his flesh previewed Christ's death and the piercing of his side for the life of his bride (Rev 19:7). Falk, *Coming to Peace with Science*, 221.

54. Irons and Kline, "The Framework View," 238.

55. Henri Blocher, *In the Beginning: The Opening Chapters of Genesis* (Downers Grove, Ill.: InterVarsity, 1984), 133.

56. Brown, "Reconciling Scientific and Biblical Portraits," 224.

57. "Commenting on whether the human author of Genesis 2 intended a literal reading of the story of Eve being crafted from the side of Adam, Henri Blocher says, 'But the presence of one or several word-plays casts doubt on any literal intention on the author's part; they reveal an author who is in no way naïve, but who uses naïve language for calculated effects' [Blocher 1984, 98–99]. Similarly, Gordon Wenham comments that 'Indeed, the whole account [of] woman's creation has a poetic flavor: it is certainly mistaken to read it as an account of a clinical operation or as an attempt to explain some feature of a man's anatomy' [Wenham 1987, 1:69]." Howard J. Van Till, "The Fully Gifted Creation: Conclusion," in *Three Views of Creation and Evolution*, ed. J. P. Moreland and John Mark Reynolds (Grand Rapids, Mich.: Zondervan, 1999), 243.

58. Polkinghorne, *Exploring Reality*, 46.

59. Barbour, *Religion and Science*, 255.

60. Brown, "Reconciling Scientific and Biblical Portraits," 221.

61. Millard J. Erickson, *Christian Theology* (Grand Rapids, Mich.: Baker, 1985), 1175.

62. Nancey Murphy, *Bodies and Souls, or Spirited Bodies?* Current Issues in Theology (Cambridge: Cambridge University Press, 2006), 57.

63. I've heard it described that the soul is "that aspect of ourselves that God sees," and thus mental capacity is irrelevant. This is an important caveat when speaking of the mentally ill and disabled. Theology opposes any attempt to label someone with mentally deficiencies as less human or devoid of dignity.

64. Jürgen Moltmann, *God in Creation: An Ecological Doctrine of Creation* (Minneapolis, Minn.: Fortress, 1993), 77.

65. I know that this may suggest that I am what's called an "annihilationist," but I'm not prepared to go that far. Jesus does mention "eternal punishment" in Matt 25:46, though it may be that the complete annihilation of an eternal being is punishment enough.

6. God Is Great, God Is Good—but Maybe I've Misunderstood?

1. This paragraph summarizes parts of Robin Marantz Henig, "Darwin's God," *New York Times Magazine* n.v. (March 4, 2007): 36–85.

2. Approximately four percent of the matter of the universe is visible matter. Richard Panek, "Out There," *New York Times Magazine* n.v. (March 11, 2007): 56.

3. Ibid.

4. Haught, *God after Darwin*, 5.

5. Russell, "Special Providence and Genetic Mutation," 366.

6. Polkinghorne, *Exploring Reality*, 141.

7. Nancey Murphy, "Nature's God," *Christian Century* 122, no. 26 (December 27, 2005): 25.

8. Barbour, *Religion and Science*, 235.

9. Derek Kidner, *Genesis: An Introduction and Commentary* (TOTC n.v.; Downers Grove, Ill.: InterVarsity, 1967), 26.

10. Joel B. Green, "Resurrection of the Body: New Testament Voices Concerning Personal Continuity and the Afterlife," in *What About the Soul? Neuroscience and Christian Anthropology*, ed. Joel B. Green (Nashville: Abingdon, 2004), 86.

11. Nancey Murphy, "Human Nature: Historical, Scientific and Religious Issues," in *Whatever Happened to the Soul? Scientific and Theological Portraits of Human Nature*, ed. Warren S. Brown, Nancey Murphy, and H. Newton Malony (Minneapolis: Fortress, 1998), 1.

12. Polkinghorne, *Exploring Reality*, 47.

13. Wolfhart Pannenberg, *Systematic Theology*, trans. Geoffrey W. Bromiley; 3 vols. (Grand Rapids, Mich.: Eerdmans, 1998), 3:601.

7. Sunday Lunch

1. This notion of Sunday lunch was borrowed with gratitude from a Sunday lunch in 2002 with the Rev. Peter Gomes.

2. Mary Higby Schweitzer et al., "Analyses of Soft Tissue from *Tyrannosaurus rex* Suggest the Presence of Protein," *Science* 316, no. 5822 (April 13, 2007): 277–80.

3. Francisco J. Ayala and Mario Coluzzi, "Chromosome Speciation: Humans, Drosophila and Mosquitoes," *PNAS* 102 (May 3, 2005): 6535–42, http://www.pnas.org/cgi/content/full/102/suppl_1/6535 (accessed June 20, 2007).

4. Gilbert Waldbauer, *What Good Are Bugs? Insects in the Web of Life* (Cambridge, Mass.: Harvard University Press, 2003), 224.

5. See p. 42.

6. Polkinghorne, *Exploring Reality*, 14.

7. Murphy, "Nature's God," 26.

8. C. S. Lewis, *The Problem of Pain* (New York: Macmillan, 1962), 28.

9. Peacocke, *Evolution*, 13.

10. In this vein, many quote Tennyson's "In Memoriam": "Who trusted God was love indeed / And love Creation's final law— / Tho' Nature, red in tooth and claw / With ravine, shriek'd against his creed—" (frag. 56).

11. Laurie J. Braaten, "May the Glory of the Lord Endure Forever! Biblical Reflections on Creation Care," in *Perspectives on an Evolving Creation*, ed. Keith B. Miller (Grand Rapids, Mich.: Eerdmans, 2003), 433.

12. Irons and Kline, "The Framework Reply," 286–88.

13. Haught, *God after Darwin*, 130.

14. Ibid.

15. McGrath, *The Science of God*, 44.

16. Warren S. Brown, "Cognitive Contributions to Soul," in *Whatever Happened to the Soul? Scientific and Theological Portraits of Human Nature*, ed. Warren S. Brown, Nancey Murphy, and H. Newton Malony (Minneapolis, Minn.: Fortress, 1998), 103.

17. Ibid., 124–25.

18. *Cartesian* refers to Rene Descartes (1596–1650) of "I think therefore I am" fame.

19. Malcolm Jeeves, "Brain, Mind and Behavior," in *Whatever Happened to the Soul? Scientific and Theological Portraits of Human Nature*, ed. Warren S. Brown, Nancey Murphy, and H. Newton Malony (Minneapolis: Fortress, 1998), 89.

20. Brown, "Cognitive Contributions to Soul," 100.

21. Polkinghorne, *Exploring Reality*, 22.

22. Lawson G. Stone, "The Soul: Possession, Part or Person? The Genesis of Human Nature in Genesis 2:7," in *What About the Soul? Neuroscience and Christian Anthropology*, ed. Joel B. Green (Nashville: Abingdon, 2004), 50–51.

23. That is only if we can say that Adam and Eve evolved as the first among *Homo sapiens*, specially chosen by God for personal relationship with him (see ch. 5). Another way around this evolutionary conundrum is to suggest that Adam and Eve, as historical persons, were neither the first sinners, nor the first humans. "They were earthly. Created of the dust of the earth (that is, they came from an earthly line of fallen humanity). But they received a new spirit because God wished to counteract the Satan-blighted creation. They were unique in that God took them out from sinful humanity, placed them in a perfect environment, and commanded them to care for the garden and avoid the tree of the knowledge of good and evil. But like their fathers and mothers before them, they willfully chose disobedience instead of righteousness and eternal life." Hurd, "Hominids in the Garden?" 226. The problem, of course, is that Genesis describes Adam and Eve as the first sinners.

24. While for Augustine and the Western church, human perfection was realized in paradise before the entry of sin, for Irenaeus and much of Eastern tradition, humanity was created perfect only in a potential sense. Murphy, "Christology, Evolution and the Cross," 382.

8. Peach Pie in the Sky

1. Ross and Archer, "The Day-Age View," 132.

2. Robin Collins, "Evolution and Original Sin," in *Perspectives on an Evolving Creation*, ed. Keith B. Miller (Grand Rapids, Mich.: Eerdmans, 2003), 486.

3. Stone, "The Soul," 60.

4. John Milbank, *Being Reconciled: Ontology and Pardon* (New York: Routledge, 2003), 17–18.

5. Ibid.

6. Russell, "Special Providence and Genetic Mutation," 367.

7. Haught, *God after Darwin*, 38.

8. Murphy, "Christology, Evolution and the Cross," 380.

9. Irons and Kline, "The Framework View," 238.

10. Based on conversation with Dr. Richard Kearney, Professor of Philosophy, Boston College, 2007.

11. Blocher, *In the Beginning*, 191.

12. Clark Pinnock et al. *The Openness of God: A Biblical Challenge to the Traditional Understanding of God* (Downers Grove, Ill.: InterVarsity, 1994), n.p.

13. It's customary to think that we move from the past *to* the future, but time itself moves *from* the future past us. One of the real conundrums of physics and philosophy is to speak of what is exactly meant by "the present" (since as soon as you even say it, it's already the past).

14. Russell and Wegter-McNelly, "Natural Law and Divine Action," 50–51.

15. Ibid.

16. Hawking, *A Brief History of Time*, 21.

17. Charles E. Gutenson, "Time, Eternity and Personal Identity: The Implications of Trinitarian Theology," in *What About the Soul? Neuroscience and Christian Anthropology*, ed. Joel B. Green (Nashville: Abingdon, 2004), 120.

18. Polkinghorne, "The Inbuilt Potentiality of Creation," 259.

19. Haught, *God after Darwin*, 46.

20. Moltmann, *God in Creation*, 82–83.

21. Barbour, *Religion and Science*, 330.

22. Moltmann, *God in Creation*, 90.

23. Pannenberg, *Systematic Theology*, 3:607.

24. Collins, "Evolution and Original Sin," 484.

25. Pannenberg, *Systematic Theology*, 3:605–6.

26. Bill T. Arnold, "Soul-Searching Questions about 1 Samuel 28: Samuel's Appearance at Endor and Christian Anthropology," in *What About the Soul? Neuroscience and Christian Anthropology*, 83.

27. Ibid., 122.

28. Dr. Gordon Hugenberger rightly reminds that Christ's resurrection occurred *within* time. Should we not therefore assume that our own will likewise happen in time? Perhaps. Though the ascension of Jesus seems to suggest a distinction between the temporal resurrection appearances of Jesus on earth in time (a miraculous event for the sake of vindicating Christ as Savior) and the atemporal seating of Christ in heaven where he is no longer confined in time. Though as God, Jesus is already seated in eternity even as he temporarily appears on earth.

29. Dr. Walter Kim rightly wonders how I would explain the Old Testament presentation of Sheol or the Revelation saints who petition God. Both suggest an intermediate state after death. If they are in block time existence, why do they act as if they are stuck

in flowing time reality? My answer is that theologically speaking, block universe "time" and flowing time are not mutually exclusive. Here, "already-not-yet" is applied post-mortem. The saints petition God to act to bring final justice and the close of time, *especially* because they now know the glorious outcome.

30. Haught, *God after Darwin*, 39.

BIBLIOGRAPHY

Arnold, Bill T. "Soul-Searching Questions about 1 Samuel 28: Samuel's Appearance at Endor and Christian Anthropology." Pages 75-84 in *What about the Soul: Neuroscience and Christian Anthropology*. Edited by Joel B. Green. Nashville: Abingdon, 2004.

Ayala, Francisco J. "Design without Designer: Darwin's Greatest Discovery." Pages 55–80 in *Debating Design: From Darwin to DNA*. Edited by William A. Dembski and Michael Ruse. Cambridge: Cambridge University Press, 2006.

Ayala, Francisco J., and Mario Coluzzi. "Chromosome Speciation: Humans, Drosophila and Mosquitoes." *Proceedings of the National Academy of Sciences of the United States of America* 102 (3 May 2005): 6535–42. http://www.pnas.org/cgi/content/full/102/suppl_1/6535 (accessed June 20, 2007).

Barbour, Ian G. *Religion and Science: Historical and Contemporary Issues*. New York: HarperSanFrancisco, 1997.

Blocher, Henri. *In the Beginning: The Opening Chapters of Genesis*. Downers Grove, Ill.: InterVarsity, 1984.

Bloom, Paul. "Is God an Accident?" *Atlantic Monthly* 296, no. 5 (December 2005): 105–12.

Braaten, Laurie J. "May the Glory of the Lord Endure Forever! Biblical Reflections on Creation Care." Pages 414–34 in *Perspectives on an Evolving Creation*. Edited by Keith B. Miller. Grand Rapids, Mich.: Eerdmans, 2003.

Bradley, Walter L. "Information, Entropy and the Origin of Life." Pages 331–51 in *Debating Design: From Darwin to DNA*. Edited by William A. Dembski and Michael Ruse. Cambridge: Cambridge University Press, 2006.

Brown, Warren S. "Cognitive Contributions to Soul." Pages 99–125 in *Whatever Happened to the Soul? Scientific and Theological Portrait of Human Nature*. Edited by Warren S. Brown, Nancey Murphy, and H. Newton Malony. Minneapolis, Minn.: Fortress, 1998.

Brown, Warren S. "Reconciling Scientific and Biblical Portraits of Human Nature." Pages 213–28 in *Whatever Happened to the Soul? Scientific and Theological Portraits of Human Nature*. Edited by Warren S. Brown, Nancey Murphy, and H. Newton Malony. Minneapolis, Minn.: Fortress, 1998.

Campbell, David, and Keith B. Miller. "The 'Cambrian Explosion': A Challenge to Evolutionary Theory?" Pages 182–204 in *Perspectives on an Evolving Creation*. Edited by Keith B. Miller. Grand Rapids, Mich.: Eerdmans, 2003.

BIBLIOGRAPHY

Caputo, John. *Philosophy and Theology*. Nashville: Abingdon, 2006.

Coakley, Sarah. "A New Way of Looking at God and Evolution." *Harvard Divinity Bulletin* 35, nos. 2 and 3 (Spring/Summer 2007): 8–13.

Collins, Francis S. *The Language of God: A Scientist Presents Evidence for Belief.* New York: Free, 2006.

Collins, Robin. "Evolution and Original Sin." Pages 469–501 in *Perspectives on an Evolving Creation*. Edited by Keith B. Miller. Grand Rapids, Mich.: Eerdmans, 2003.

Darwin, Charles. *The Origin of Species*. 1859. Repr., Chicago: Encyclopedia Britannica, 1952.

Davis, John Jefferson. "Response to Howard J. Van Till." Pages 226–30 in *Three Views of Creation and Evolution*. Edited by J. P. Moreland and John Mark Reynolds. Grand Rapids, Mich.: Zondervan, 1999.

Dennett, Daniel C. *Breaking the Spell: Religion as Natural Phenomenon*. New York: Viking, 2006.

Edwards, Denis. *The God of Evolution*. New York: Paulist, 1999.

Erickson, Millard J. *Christian Theology*. Grand Rapids, Mich.: Baker, 1985.

Fackre, Gabriel. *The Christian Story*. 3rd ed. Grand Rapids, Mich.: Eerdmans, 1996.

Falk, Darrel R. *Coming to Peace with Science: Bridging the Worlds between Faith and Biology*. Downers Grove, Ill.: InterVarsity, 2004.

Gingerich, Owen. *God's Universe*. Cambridge, Mass.: The Belknap Press of Harvard University Press, 2006.

Gould, Stephen Jay. *The Structure of Evolutionary Theory*. Cambridge, Mass.: Harvard University Press, 2002.

Green, Joel B. "Resurrection of the Body: New Testament Voices Concerning Personal Continuity and the Afterlife." Pages 85–100 in *What About the Soul? Neuroscience and Christian Anthropology*. Edited by Joel B. Green. Nashville: Abingdon, 2004.

Greene, Brian. *The Elegant Universe: Superstrings, Hidden Dimensions and the Quest for the Ultimate Theory*. New York: Norton, 2003.

Grenz, Stanley J. *Theology for the Community of God*. Nashville: Broadman & Holman, 1994.

Gutenson, Charles E. "Time, Eternity and Personal Identity: The Implications of Trinitarian Theology." Pages 117–32 in *What About the Soul? Neuroscience and Christian Anthropology*. Edited by Joel B. Green. Nashville: Abingdon, 2004.

Haarsma, Deborah B., and Jennifer Wiseman. "An Evolving Cosmos." Pages 97–119 in *Perspectives on an Evolving Creation*. Edited by Keith B. Miller. Grand Rapids, Mich.: Eerdmans, 2003.

Haarsma, Loren. "Does Science Exclude God? Natural Law, Chance, Miracles and Scientific Practice." Pages 72–96 in *Perspectives on an Evolving Creation*. Edited by Keith B. Miller. Grand Rapids, Mich.: Eerdmans, 2003.

Haarsma, Loren, and Terry M. Gray. "Complexity, Self-Organization and Design." Pages 288–312 in *Perspectives on an Evolving Creation*. Edited by Keith B. Miller. Grand Rapids, Mich.: Eerdmans, 2003.

Harrell, Daniel. "A Day at the Genetic Circus." *Regeneration Quarterly* 5, no. 3 (Fall 1999): 10–11.

Haught, John F. "Darwin, Design and Divine Providence." Pages 229–45 in *Debating Design: From Darwin to DNA*. Edited by William A. Dembski and Michael Ruse. Cambridge: Cambridge University Press, 2006.

Haught, John F. *God after Darwin: A Theology of Evolution*. Boulder Colo.: Westview, 2000.

Hawking, Stephen W. *A Brief History of Time*. New York Bantam, 1996.

Henig, Robin Marantz. "Darwin's God." *New York Times Magazine* n.v. (4 March 2007): 36–85.

Hewlett, Martinez J. "Biological Evolution in Science and Theology." Pages 69–79 in *Bridging Science and Religion*. Edited by Ted Peters and Gaymon Bennett. Minneapolis, Minn.: Fortress, 2003.

Hoekema, Anthony A. *The Bible and the Future*. Grand Rapids Mich.: Eerdmans, 1979

Holt, Jim. "Unstrung." *New Yorker* n.v. (2 October 2006): n.p., http //www.newyorker. com/archive/2006/10/02/061002crat_atlarge (accessed June 20, 2007).

Hurd, James P. "Hominids in the Garden?" Pages 208–33 in *Perspectives on an Evolving Creation*. Edited by Keith B. Miller. Grand Rapids, Mich.: Eerdmans, 2003.

Hyers, Conrad. "Comparing Biblical and Scientific Maps of Origins." Pages 19–33 in *Perspectives on an Evolving Creation*. Edited by Keith B. Miller. Grand Rapids, Mich.: Eerdmans, 2003.

Irons, Lee, and Meredith G. Kline. "The Framework Reply." Pages 279–303 in *The Genesis Debate: Three Views on the Days of Creation*. Edited by David G. Hagopian. Mission Viejo, Calif.: Crux, 2001.

Irons, Lee, and Meredith G. Kline. "The Framework Response to the Day-Age View." Pages 179–88 in *The Genesis Debate: Three Views on the Days of Creation*. Edited by David G. Hagopian. Mission Viejo, Calif.: Crux, 2001.

Irons, Lee, and Meredith G. Kline. "The Framework View." Pages 217–56 in *The Genesis Debate: Three Views on the Days of Creation*. Edited by David G. Hagopian. Mission Viejo, Calif.: Crux, 2001.

Jeeves, Malcolm. "Brain, Mind and Behavior." Pages 73–98 in *Whatever Happened to the Soul? Scientific and Theological Portraits of Human Nature*. Edited by Warren S. Brown, Nancey Murphy, and H. Newton Malony. Minneapolis: Fortress, 1998.

Johnson, George. "Oh for the Simple Days of the Big Bang." *New York Times*, October 8, 2006, late edition, sec. 4.

Kauffman, Stuart. "Prolegomenon to a General Biology." Pages 151–72 in *Debating Design: From Darwin to DNA*. Edited by William A. Dembski and Michael Ruse. Cambridge: Cambridge University Press, 2006.

Kidner, Derek. *Genesis: An Introduction and Commentary*. Tyndale Old Testament Commentaries n.v. Downers Grove, Ill.: InterVarsity, 1967.

Kirschner, Mark W., and John C. Gerhart. *The Plausibility of Life*. New Haven, Conn.: Yale University Press, 2005.

Lewis, C. S. *The Problem of Pain*. New York: Macmillan, 1962.

Livingstone, David N. *Darwin's Forgotten Defenders: The Encounter between Evangelical Theology and Evolutionary Thought*. Grand Rapids, Mich.: Eerdmans, 1987.

Mayr, Ernst. *What Evolution Is*. New York: Basic, 2001.

McGrath, Alister E. *The Science of God: An Introduction to Scientific Theology*. London: T&T Clark, 2004.

Meilander, Gilbert. "Begetting and Cloning." *First Things* 74 (June/July 1997): 41–43.

Milbank, John. *Being Reconciled: Ontology and Pardon*. New York: Routledge, 2003.

Miller, Keith B. "An Evolving Creation: Oxymoron or Fruitful Insight?" Pages 3–14 in *Perspectives on an Evolving Creation*. Edited by Keith B. Miller. Grand Rapids, Mich.: Eerdmans, 2003.

Miller, Kenneth R. *Finding Darwin's God: A Scientist's Search for Common Ground between God and Evolution*. New York: Harper Perennial, 1999.

Moltmann, Jürgen. *God in Creation: An Ecological Doctrine of Creation.* Minneapolis Fortress, 1993.

Murphy, George L. "Christology, Evolution and the Cross." Pages 370–89 in *Perspectives on an Evolving Creation.* Edited by Keith B. Miller. Grand Rapids, Mich.: Eerdmans, 2003.

Murphy, Nancey. *Anglo-American Postmodernity: Philosophical Perspectives on Science, Religion and Ethics.* Boulder, Colo.: Westview, 1997.

Murphy, Nancey. *Bodies and Souls, or Spirited Bodies?* Current Issues in Theology. Cambridge: Cambridge University Press, 2006.

Murphy, Nancey. "Human Nature: Historical, Scientific and Religious Issues." Pages 1–30 in *Whatever Happened to the Soul? Scientific and Theological Portraits of Human Nature.* Edited by Warren S. Brown, Nancey Murphy, and H. Newton Malony. Minneapolis: Fortress, 1998.

Murphy, Nancey. "Nature's God." *Christian Century* 122, no. 26 (27 December 2005): 20–22, 24–28.

Noll, Mark. *The Scandal of the Evangelical Mind.* Grand Rapids, Mich.: Eerdmans, 1994.

Panek, Richard. "Out There." *New York Times Magazine* n.v. (11 March 2007): 55–56.

Pannenberg, Wolfhart. *Systematic Theology.* Translated by Geoffrey W. Bromiley. 3 vols. Grand Rapids, Mich.: Eerdmans, 1998.

Particle Data Group. "What Holds It Together? Strong," http://particleadventure.org/frameless/strong.html (accessed June 20, 2007).

Peacocke, Arthur R. *Evolution: The Disguised Friend of Faith?* Philadelphia: Templeton, 2004.

Petersen, Dan. "What's the Big Deal about Intelligent Design?" *American Spectator,* December 22, 2005. http://spectator.org/.

Pinker, Steven. *How the Mind Works.* New York: Norton, 1997.

Pinnock, Clark, et al. *The Openness of God: A Biblical Challenge to the Traditional Understanding of God.* Downers Grove, Ill.: InterVarsity, 1994.

Polkinghorne, John. *Belief in God in an Age of Science.* New Haven, Conn.: Yale University Press, 1998.

Polkinghorne, John. *Exploring Reality: The Intertwining of Science and Religion.* New Haven, Conn.: Yale University Press, 2005.

Polkinghorne, John. "The Inbuilt Potentiality of Creation." Pages 246–60 in *Debating Design: From Darwin to DNA.* Edited by William A. Dembski and Michael Ruse. Cambridge: Cambridge University Press, 2006.

Pollan, Michael. "Unhappy Meals." *New York Times Magazine* n.v. (28 January 2007): 38–70.

Rimas, Andrew. "He Landed the Fish That Landed Itself." *Boston Globe,* May 22, 2006, sec. C.

"RNA: Really New Advances." *Economist* 383, no. 8533 (16 June 2007), 87–89.

Ross, Hugh, and Gleason L. Archer. "The Day-Age Reply." Pages 189–214 in *The Genesis Debate: Three Views on the Days of Creation.* Edited by David G. Hagopian. Mission Viejo, Calif.: Crux, 2001.

Ross, Hugh, and Gleason L. Archer. "The Day-Age View." Pages 123–63 in *The Genesis Debate: Three Views on the Days of Creation.* Edited by David G. Hagopian. Mission Viejo, Calif.: Crux, 2001.

Roughgarden, Joan. *Evolution and Christian Faith: Reflections of an Evolutionary Biologist.* Washington, D.C.: Island, 2006.

Russell, Robert John. "Special Providence and Genetic Mutation: A New Defense of Theistic Evolution." Pages 335–69 in *Perspectives on an Evolving Creation.* Edited by Keith B. Miller. Grand Rapids, Mich.: Eerdmans, 2003.

Russell, Robert John, and Kirk Wegter-McNelly. "Natural Law and Divine Action." Pages 49–68 in *Bridging Science and Religion.* Edited by Ted Peters and Gaymon Bennett. Minneapolis: Fortress, 2003.

Ryan, Frank. *Darwin's Blind Spot: Evolution Beyond Natural Selection.* Boston: Houghton Mifflin, 2002.

Sailhamer, John H., "Genesis." Pages 3–284. *The Expositor's Bible Commentary.* Edited by Frank E. Gaebelein. Grand Rapids, Mich.: Zondervan, 1990.

Schweitzer, Mary Higby, et al. "Analyses of Soft Tissue from *Tyrannosaurus rex* Suggest the Presence of Protein." *Science* 316, no. 5822 (13 April 2007): 277–80.

Stone, Lawson G. "The Soul: Possession, Part or Person? The Genesis of Human Nature in Genesis 2:7." Pages 47–62 in *What About the Soul? Neuroscience and Christian Anthropology.* Edited by Joel B. Green. Nashville: Abingdon, 2004.

Taylor, Barbara Brown. *The Luminous Web: Essays on Science and Religion.* Boston: Cowley, 2000.

BIBLIOGRAPHY

Van Till, Howard J. "The Fully Gifted Creation: Conclusion." Pages 240–47 in *Three Views of Creation and Evolution*. Edited by J. P. Moreland and John Mark Reynolds. Grand Rapids, Mich.: Zondervan, 1999.

Van Till, Howard J. "The Fully Gifted Creation: Theistic Evolution." Pages 159–218 in *Three Views of Creation and Evolution*. Edited by J. P. Moreland and John Mark Reynolds. Grand Rapids, Mich.: Zondervan, 1999.

Van Till, Howard J. "Is the Universe Capable of Evolving?" Pages 313–34 in *Perspectives on an Evolving Creation*. Edited by Keith B. Miller. Grand Rapids, Mich.: Eerdmans, 2003.

Waldbauer, Gilbert. *What Good Are Bugs? Insects in the Web of Life*. Cambridge, Mass.: Harvard University Press, 2003.

Wenham, Gordon J. *Genesis*. 2 vols. Word Biblical Commentary 1–2. Waco, Tex.: Word Books, 1987.

Wenham, Gordon J. "Genesis." Pages 54–91 in *The New Bible Commentary: 21st Century Edition*. 4th ed. Edited by D. A. Carson et al. Downers Grove, Ill.: InterVarsity, 1994.

Wilcox, David L. "Finding Adam: The Genetics of Human Origins ' Pages 234–53 in *Perspectives on an Evolving Creation*. Edited by Keith B. Miller. Grand Rapids, Mich.: Eerdmans, 2003.

Wilson, Edward O. *Consilience: The Unity of Knowledge*. New York: Knopf, 1999.

Subject Index

SCRIPTURE INDEX